APPLIED COMMUNICATION SKILLS

Writing Paragraphs

CAMBRIDGE ADULT EDUCATION
A Division of Simon & Schuster
Upper Saddle River, New Jersey

Executive Editor: Mark Moscowitz
Project Editors: Karen Bernhaut, Douglas Falk, Amy Jolin, Kris Shepos-Salvatore
Production Editor: Alan Dalgleish
Marketing Manager: Will Jarred
Series Editor: Mary McGarry
Consulting Editor: Michael Buchman
Interior Design and Electronic Page Production: Pencil Point Studio
Cover Design: Pat Smythe, Marjory Dressler

Writer: Betsy Feist

Copyright © 1996 by Cambridge Adult Education, a division of
Simon & Schuster, One Lake Street, Upper Saddle River, New Jersey 07458.
All rights reserved. No part of this book may be reproduced or transmitted
in any form or by any means, electrical or mechanical, including photocopying,
recording, or by any information storage and retrieval system, without
permission in writing from the publisher.

Printed in the United States of America

1 2 3 4 5 6 7 8 9 10   99 98 97 96 95

ISBN 0-835-91915-3

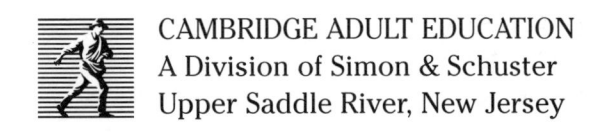

CAMBRIDGE ADULT EDUCATION
A Division of Simon & Schuster
Upper Saddle River, New Jersey

CONTENTS

CHAPTER 1   GETTING READY TO WRITE PARAGRAPHS 1
    LESSON 1: Getting the Facts Straight 3
    LESSON 2: The Structure of a Paragraph 6
    For Your Portfolio: Begin a Writing Portfolio 9

CHAPTER 2:   FOCUSING YOUR TOPIC 10
    LESSON 1: Purpose 12
    LESSON 2: Audience 14
    LESSON 3: Topic Sentence 17
    For Your Portfolio: Write a Paragraph To Reach
                            Your Audience and Achieve a Purpose 20

CHAPTER 3:   SUPPORTING SENTENCES 21
    LESSON 1: Brainstorming 23
    LESSON 2: Clustering 25
    LESSON 3: Organizing Ideas 27
    For Your Portfolio: Gather and Organize Ideas for a Paragraph 31

CHAPTER 4:   CONCLUDING SENTENCE 32
    LESSON 1: Content and Placement
                  of a Concluding Sentence 34
    LESSON 2: Unity 38
    For Your Portfolio: Write a Paragraph
                            with a Strong Conclusion 40

CHAPTER 5:   KINDS OF PARAGRAPHS:
               INFORMATIVE, DESCRIPTIVE, NARRATIVE 41
    LESSON 1: Paragraphs that Inform 43
    LESSON 2: Paragraphs that Describe 46
    LESSON 3: Narrative Paragraphs 49
    For Your Portfolio: Write Three Kinds of Paragraphs 51

CHAPTER 6:   KINDS OF PARAGRAPHS: PERSUASIVE 52
    LESSON 1: Writing to Persuade 54
    LESSON 2: Writing to Complain 57
    LESSON 3: Writing to Threaten Action 59
    For Your Portfolio: Persuade People to Act 61

CHAPTER 7: **KINDS OF CORRESPONDENCE: MEMOS, E-MAIL, FAXES, AND MESSAGES** 62
    LESSON 1: Memos 64
    LESSON 2: E-Mail and Fax Communications 65
    LESSON 3: Telephone Messages 70
    For Your Portfolio: Write a Memo Outlining a Plan 73

CHAPTER 8: **KINDS OF CORRESPONDENCE: LETTERS** 74
    LESSON 1: Heading, Inside Address, and Greeting 76
    LESSON 2: The Closing of the Letter 78
    LESSON 3: Envelopes and Labels 80
    LESSON 4: Form Letters 81
    For Your Portfolio: Write a Letter 84

CHAPTER 9: **FORMS** 85
    LESSON 1: Resumes 87
    LESSON 2: Job Applications 90
    For Your Portfolio: Write a Resume 94

CHAPTER 10: **REPORTS** 95
    LESSON 1: Writing Introductory Paragraphs 98
    LESSON 2: Writing Transitional Paragraphs 99
    LESSON 3: Writing a Conclusion 101
    LESSON 4: Illustrating Reports with Tables 102
    LESSON 5: Creating Graphs for a Report 104
    For Your Portfolio: Combine Different Kinds of Paragraphs 108

CHAPTER 11: **REVISING, EDITING, AND PROOFREADING** 109
    LESSON 1: Revising 111
    LESSON 2: Editing 113
    LESSON 3: Proofreading 117
    For Your Portfolio: Draft, Revise, Edit, and Proofread a Paragraph 120

GLOSSARY 121

ANSWER KEY 129

TO THE STUDENT

Welcome to *Applied Communication Skills!* This series will help you build your communication skills: listening, speaking, reading, and writing. These communication skills are presented in realistic workplace settings, so that you can see how these skills relate to your life at work.

What This Series Teaches

Each chapter contains a series of lessons and exercises. The skills you learn and practice in these lessons and exercises will help you prepare for the GED exam.

The skills build in difficulty from book to book:

- Grammar Skills
- Spelling and Vocabulary
- Writing Sentences
- Writing Paragraphs

These books were written to make grammar, vocabulary, and writing interesting and easy. The books emphasize the basic concepts and give you exactly what you need to know to speak and write correct English. Throughout this series you will find examples of correct use and incorrect use. This will make it easy for you to see the difference between what is correct and what is not.

The workplace settings used in this series vary. They include the following vocational areas: agriculture, business, family and consumer services, health professions, marketing, technology, and trade and industry. Each of these areas has a logo that is used on the chapter opening page and at the bottom of each page to identify the workplace setting. The logos are:

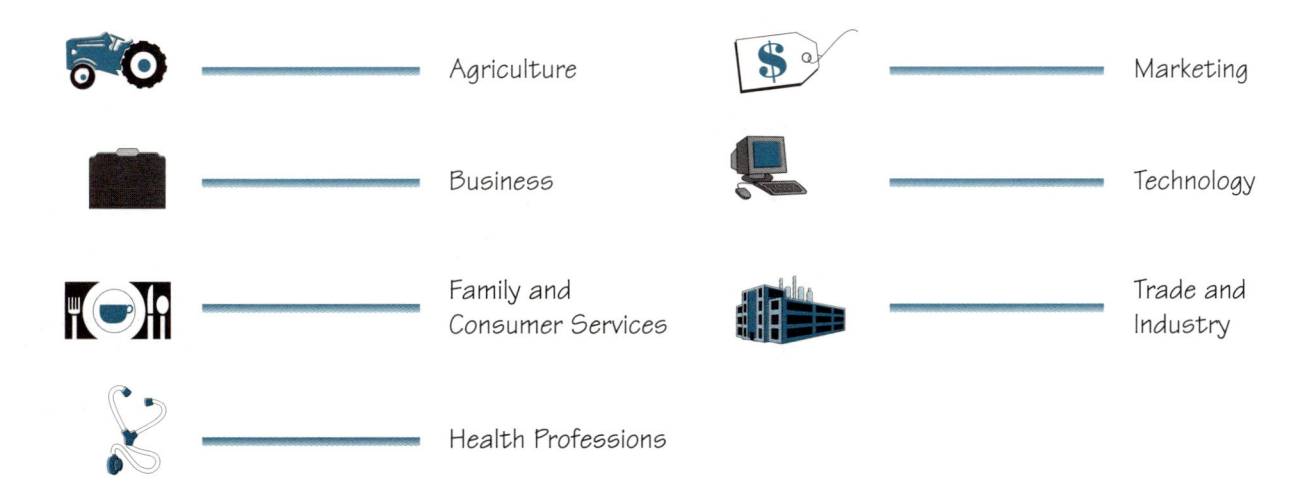

- Agriculture
- Business
- Family and Consumer Services
- Health Professions
- Marketing
- Technology
- Trade and Industry

The communication skills presented in each lesson focus on one of these seven vocational areas. As you learn the basic principles of grammar, vocabulary, and writing, you can apply these principles in the way you would at work.

How This Series Is Designed for You

Each book in this series motivates and guides your progress. In each chapter, you will:

- Read the *Words at Work* section to master the specialized work terms used in the chapter. Note that every boldface term in the chapter is defined in the Glossary at the end of the book.

- Read the opening story about a workplace problem in a section called *Solving Communication Problems*.

- Solve the communication problem in a section called *Applying Communication Skills*.

- Complete *Lessons and Exercises*. Check your answers in the *Answer Key* at the end of the book.

- Read boxed passages, called *FYI*, for helpful tips.

- Work on a continuing project in a section called *For Your Portfolio*. This project will help you build a collection of written work as you master key communication skills.

As your skills improve, your communication—both at home and at work—will become clearer and more effective. Good luck!

Mary McGarry
Series Editor

CHAPTER 1

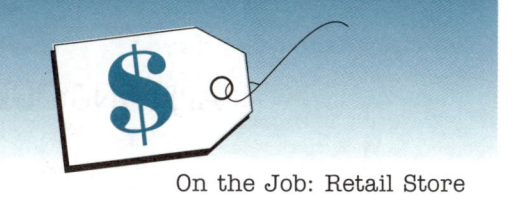

On the Job: Retail Store

Getting Ready to Write Paragraphs

SOLVING **COMMUNICATION** PROBLEMS

"What do you mean, Mrs. Custis?" said Darlene in a puzzled tone. "I'm so sorry, but I just can't figure out why you want me to write a **self appraisal**. I don't have to write on this job. So I don't see what writing an appraisal has to do with me or the raise I asked for!"

"Well, Darlene," said Mrs. Custis, "I want you to tell me how you think you are doing your job here at Peachtree Fashion Stores. Tell me what you do well and what you'd like to improve. Finally, tell me about any training you feel you need. I need it in writing because a self appraisal is part of your employee record. Once I get your self appraisal, we can sit down and discuss it. I'll give you my opinion of how well you are doing. That's called a **performance appraisal.** I also put it in writing for your employee record, and then notify Accounting to give you a raise."

"That's an awful lot of fuss for a small raise!" said Darlene angrily. "Besides, I'm not comfortable with writing. But I'm a good salesperson, and I deserve more money!"

"Don't get upset, Darlene," said Mrs. Custis. "This is the **standard procedure** that the **human relations** department set up for everyone. When you were hired, we told you that each employee gets a formal performance appraisal every year. And if you want to advance in the company, you need to get more comfortable with writing. For instance, **buyers** do lots of writing. But you only have to write a few paragraphs now for your self appraisal."

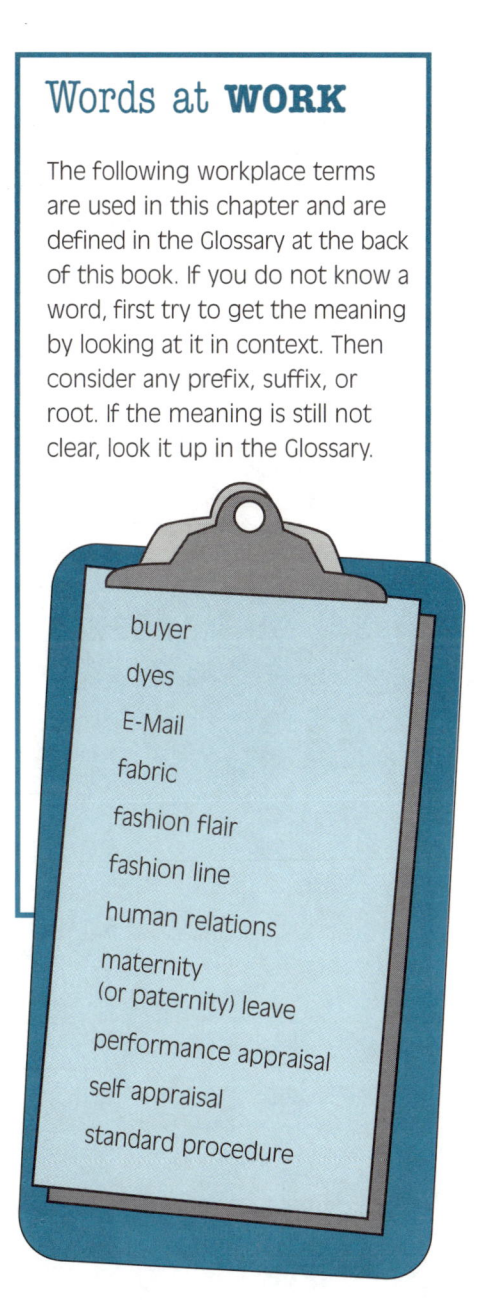

Words at **WORK**

The following workplace terms are used in this chapter and are defined in the Glossary at the back of this book. If you do not know a word, first try to get the meaning by looking at it in context. Then consider any prefix, suffix, or root. If the meaning is still not clear, look it up in the Glossary.

- buyer
- dyes
- E-Mail
- fabric
- fashion flair
- fashion line
- human relations
- maternity (or paternity) leave
- performance appraisal
- self appraisal
- standard procedure

APPLYING **COMMUNICATION** SKILLS

1. What is Darlene's main communication problem?

2. What might have caused it?

3. What are some possible solutions to the problem?

4. Select the one solution that you think is best. Why would you suggest that Darlene try it?

5. How might Darlene get help in overcoming her dislike for writing?

6. How do you feel about writing? Jot down some words and phrases that express your feelings about writing.

_____

_____

_____

_____

Check your answers on page 129.

LESSON 1 Getting the Facts Straight

For many people the hardest thing about writing on the job is not WHAT to say, but HOW to say it. Even a simple one-paragraph memo suddenly seems like a complex mix of facts, grammar, punctuation, and workplace vocabulary. A very common reaction is to freeze up and not be able to write at all!

Experienced writers offer this advice: forget about grammar, punctuation, and even vocabulary at first. Focus on answering five basic questions: WHO? WHY? WHAT? WHEN? HOW? The answers to these questions will become your paragraph.

A **paragraph** is a group of sentences that develop a single idea. We write in paragraphs to make the organization of our ideas clear to our readers. If you think about writing a paragraph as a step-by-step process, it will help you sort through the confusion. The first step of the writing process is to gather your ideas and facts.

To get the facts together for a one-paragraph message, ask yourself the following five questions:

1. WHO will read your message? Do you know the reader's name and job?

2. WHY are you writing? What result do you want from the reader? What task should the reader complete after reading your message?

3. WHAT information does your reader need to know? Put yourself in your reader's place. Then you can figure out WHAT he or she needs to know in order to do the task.

4. WHEN must the task be done? Time is often critical in business. Even if the reader is your boss, be sure to request a response by the needed time.

5. HOW should the job be done? Few people like to be told how to do their jobs. Make sure that you have the authority to direct the reader, and then do it tactfully.

Workplace Success

EXAMPLE

Let's look at a real-life example of a one-paragraph message:

E-MAIL MESSAGE   1:15 P.M.

> TO: SARA WHITE, Office Manager
> FROM: JIM CANNOLINI, Buyer Trainee in Menswear
> SUBJECT: Broken Phone
> DATE: May 2, 199X
>
> My phone broke today at about 11:30 A.M. I can get incoming calls, but I can't make outgoing ones. My extension is 2345. My boss said to put this in writing to you on **E-mail** because you are in charge of phones. Please fix it fast, because I am using Jill's phone. She gets back from vacation on May 4.

1. To whom is Jim writing? _____

2. Why is he writing? _____

3. When is the deadline for the task? _____

4. Is the HOW of Jim's message tactfully worded? If you were Sara, how would you respond to this wording?

   _____
   _____
   _____

5. What did Jim say well?

   _____
   _____

6. What did he say poorly?

   _____
   _____
   _____
   _____

Check your answers on page 129.

Chapter 1   Getting Ready to Write Paragraphs

EXERCISE 1 Who Gets the Message?

Each of the following paragraphs is intended for a specific reader. Circle the name of the person you think the paragraph addresses.

1. I am writing because my latest raise is not fair. My work is good, and I am also always on time. Many customers ask for me to help them. I would like to meet with you to review my file of notes and letters from satisfied customers.

    a. coworker   c. supervisor
    b. client   d. friend

2. Mr. Watson, I wanted to thank you again for the charming little dress that you sent me for my new baby. Mei Ling looks adorable in it! See the enclosed photo of us to judge for yourself. It's no wonder that Kidee Clothes are so popular with Peachtree customers! I'm sure that you will sell many of these dresses to stores around the country. I hope that we can work together again as soon as I return from **maternity leave.**

    a. coworker   c. supervisor
    b. friend   d. supplier

3. This is a just a quick note, Al, to ask you to follow up on a possible sale. My brother called me from Texas last night. His next-door neighbor is moving here and wants to buy uniforms for the workers in his new bike shop. Since you are in charge of uniform sales, I'm passing this on to you. Good luck!

    a. coworker   c. client
    b. relative   d. supervisor

4. Before Peachtree Fashion Stores order more uniforms with company names, we need to discuss faster delivery. Your last shipment came only one day before we had to ship it. We need more time to inspect the goods before we send them to our clients. Please phone me as soon as you can to discuss this.

    a. coworker   c. client
    b. supervisor   d. supplier

Check your answers on page 129.

EXERCISE 2 What Do You Need to Say?

The telephone on your desk, extension 2345, is broken; there is no dial tone. Like Jim Cannolini in Example 1, you need to send the office manager, Sara White, an E-mail message to get it fixed. Before you put one word on paper, think about:

1. WHO you are writing to
2. WHAT you need to say
3. WHY you want the task done
4. WHEN you need the task done.
5. (HOW to do the task does not apply in this case.)

On a piece of scrap paper, jot down the main idea you want to communicate. It is really important to get the main idea clear. Then list two or three other points you want to cover, such as when the phone broke and the exact nature of the problem. Then put yourself in Sara's place. What details would you want to know in order to get the phone fixed quickly? For example, to say "my phone is broken" is not as helpful as saying "I get no dial tone."

Now rewrite your ideas on the following lines.

Main Idea: _____

_____

Supporting Details: _____

_____

_____

_____

_____

_____

Check your answers on page 129.

LESSON 2 The Structure of a Paragraph

A paragraph has three main parts: the topic sentence, the supporting sentence, and the concluding sentence. A **topic sentence** is one that states the main idea of your message.

The topic sentence is accompanied by one or more **supporting sentences** which explain and develop your main idea. The supporting sentences make up the middle, or **body,** of a paragraph.

The supporting sentences are followed by a **concluding sentence.** The concluding sentence often summarizes or restates your message. In some kinds of writing, the concluding sentence may urge the reader to take action. Very short paragraphs may not need a conclusion. If other paragraphs follow, the last sentence of the first paragraph may lead into the main idea of the next paragraph.

Example:

Let's look at an example of a short paragraph with all three main parts. This paragraph is from an advertising piece for Flamingo Fashion Apparel, which hopes to get Peachtree Fashions to buy its **fashion line** of casual wear.

> (1) Flamingo Fashion Apparel offers the latest and best in casual wear for women. (2) We have a large selection of high fashion casual wear in a wide range of sizes, colors, and fabrics. (3) Furthermore, our award-winning designer, Yolanda Munoz, is featured in the Miami Designers of the Year Show. (4) So come to Flamingo for **fashion flair** in casual wear!

In this example, sentence 1 is the topic sentence. Sentences 2 and 3 are supporting sentences. They give us more details about Flamingo Fashion Apparel. The final sentence is the concluding sentence: it urges customers to buy Flamingo Fashion Apparel.

EXERCISE 1 Identify the Parts of a Paragraph

Using the following paragraphs from the Flamingo Fashion Apparel advertising piece, write the number of the topic sentence and the number of the conclusion.

A. (1) Our summer line features a new **fabric,** called Sunnie, that your customers will love! (2) It is called Sunnie because of its resistance to fading by sunlight. (3) Sunnie is also machine washable and doesn't wrinkle. (4) Your customers will see this new fabric in fashion magazines and on TV. (5) Be the first store in your area to offer the hottest and coolest new fabric in casual wear — Sunnie!

_____ topic sentence   _____ concluding sentence

B. (1) Sunnie takes **dyes** very well, from the palest pastels to the brightest shades. (2) This feature inspired our designer, Yolanda Munoz, to use the newest, brightest colors for the summer. (3) It comes in hot, hot colors: flamingo pink, fire engine red, parrot green, sun yellow, and bright blue. (4) Stock up now on this brand new line of bright casual wear.

_____ topic sentence   _____ concluding sentence

C. (1) We call our new line of bright casual wear the Fiesta Sol line. (2) Our Fiesta Sol line comes in a wide range of styles and sizes. (3) The line consists of 12 pieces: slacks, shorts, skirts, jackets, halters, and a number of different tee shirts. (4) Sizes range from petites through women's sizes. (5) Place your order today to get the complete Fiesta Sol line for your customers!

_____ topic sentence   _____ concluding sentence

D. (1) In addition to the Fiesta Sol line, we offer another line using Sunnie fabric called Sombra. (2) Our Sombra line features darker shades for late summer and early fall: olive green, gold, rust, and black. (3) Our Sombra line has six pieces: skirt, slacks, jacket, short sleeve dress, and two different blouses with short sleeves. (4) The Sombra line will also sell out fast, so place your orders now for August 1 delivery.

_____ topic sentence   _____ concluding sentence

Check your answers on page 129.

FYI

THE WRITING PROCESS

The writing process breaks writing into stages. Your ideas, notes, drafts, revisions, and editing lead to a polished piece of work. The writing process has five stages:

1. **Prewriting** is what you do before you write. This is the planning stage. It is the time to think about why you are writing, what you need to say, how you will get your point across, and who will read your writing.

2. **Drafting** is the stage when you bring all of your information together into a readable form. If your planning has been thorough, the drafting stage can go as quickly as you can write. Don't worry about how your writing looks or sounds. Your goal in drafting is to get your thoughts down on paper as completely as possible.

3. **Revising** is the stage when you look closely at what you have written and try to improve it. You may have to rearrange your ideas, add details, or even cut some of what you have written.

4. **Editing** is polishing your writing. This is when you check your grammar, punctuation, and spelling.

5. **Publishing** is sharing your writing with another person or people. It's when you hand in your paper, file a report, or mail a letter.

FOR YOUR Portfolio

BEGIN A WRITING PORTFOLIO

Begin to collect all the writing assignments that you do for this book into a file folder. Label the folder "Writing Portfolio." By the time you reach the end of this book, you will have finished at least a dozen writing assignments. You will be surprised and pleased by how much you have written and how much you have improved. You will find that the more you write, the more comfortable you will be with the writing process.

Your first assignment is to write four simple sentences about how you feel about writing. Look back at the words and phrases you wrote down on page 3. Rewrite these words and phrases in complete sentences.

Try to put your main idea in the first sentence, your supporting ideas in the next two sentences, and your conclusion in the last sentence. Don't forget to read over what you have written.

Workplace Success

CHAPTER 2

On the Job: Retail Store

Focusing Your Topic

SOLVING **COMMUNICATION** PROBLEMS

Darlene was folding a blouse that a customer had just purchased, when Mrs. Paracha, one of her regular customers, entered the shop. Darlene smiled and nodded to let Mrs. Paracha know she would be right with her. Then she finished wrapping the package for her other customer. When she turned to greet Mrs. Paracha, she found that Rosie was showing her one of the dresses that had arrived last week.

Darlene was angry, but she tried not to let it show. After Mrs. Paracha left, Darlene approached Rosie.

"You know I always help Mrs. Paracha," Darlene told her.

"Well, you were busy with someone else," Rosie replied, "And anyway, why should you have all the best customers?"

"They ask for me," Darlene said, "because I remember the kinds of things they like, and I help them make good purchases. I'm sure that if I had waited on Mrs. Paracha, she would not have left empty-handed."

The hard feelings lasted throughout the rest of the day. At closing time, Darlene and Rosie were still giving each other cold looks.

"What's the matter?" Mrs. Custis asked, "Why are the two of you in such a state?"

"She stole my customer," Darlene said, glaring at Rosie.

Rosie glared right back, and said, "Why should she get all the good customers? She probably makes ten times as much as I do in **commission**. And I'm the one with a child to support. She's probably spending all that commission money on earrings—she seems to wear new ones every day. Meanwhile, I've got to scrimp to pay the baby-sitter."

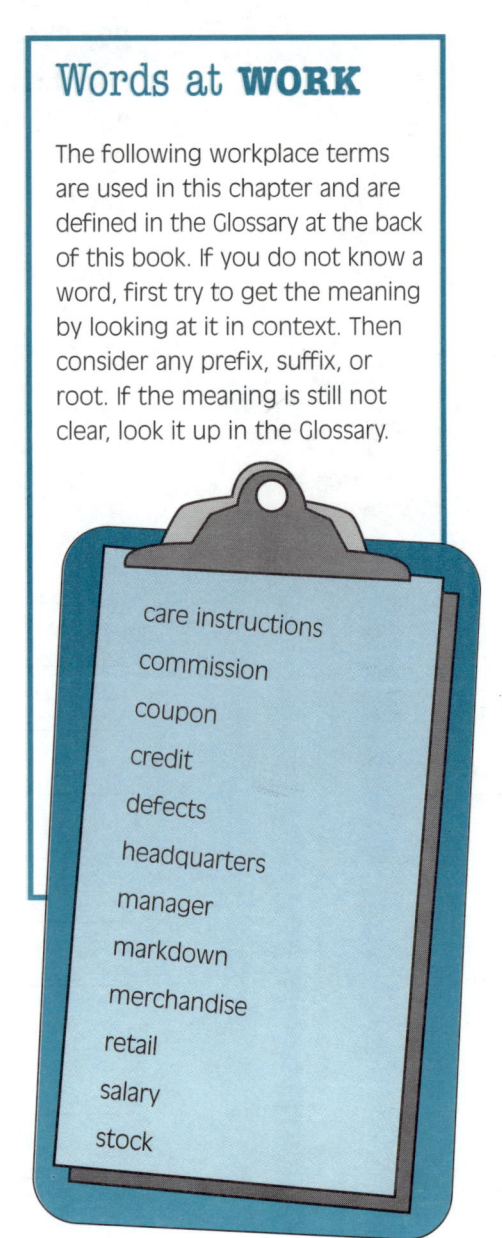

Words at **WORK**

The following workplace terms are used in this chapter and are defined in the Glossary at the back of this book. If you do not know a word, first try to get the meaning by looking at it in context. Then consider any prefix, suffix, or root. If the meaning is still not clear, look it up in the Glossary.

- care instructions
- commission
- coupon
- credit
- defects
- headquarters
- manager
- markdown
- merchandise
- retail
- salary
- stock

Mrs. Custis hushed her two salespeople. "Come on, you two," she said, "it's no good for anybody if you behave like this. If you cooperate instead of competing, it will be better for the store, and better for all of us in the long run."

APPLYING **COMMUNICATION** SKILLS

Write your answers to the following questions.

1. What is the main communication problem between Darlene and Rosie?

   _____
   _____

2. What might have caused it?

   _____
   _____
   _____
   _____

3. What are some possible solutions to the problem?

   _____
   _____
   _____
   _____
   _____
   _____

4. Select the one solution you think is best. Why would you suggest that Darlene and Rosie try it?

   _____
   _____
   _____
   _____
   _____

5. Why do you think Darlene has an easier time winning loyal customers than Rosie does?

_____

_____

_____

_____

Check your answers on page 129.

LESSON 1 Purpose

The **topic** of a paragraph is its general subject. For example, you might write about the topic, "new spring fashions." When you write on the job, you usually know what your topic will be from the start. What you say about the topic largely depends upon your purpose for writing. Your specific purpose is likely to fall into one of five categories:

1. *To explain something.* You might write a paragraph to explain why certain dresses are in fashion this spring.

2. *To persuade your readers to do or think something.* You might write a paragraph to persuade your customers to purchase new dresses in this fashion line.

3. *To compare two things.* You might compare this spring's fashions with last spring's fashions.

4. *To describe something.* You might simply want to describe what this spring's fashions look like.

5. *To give your opinion about something.* You might write about why you like or dislike this spring's fashions.

Defining your purpose helps you choose the information you need before you start writing.

EXAMPLE

Let's look at two paragraphs on the same topic. Notice how different their purposes are.

Paragraph 1

This year's preholiday sale is going to be very different from last year's. Last year, we gave a **markdown** of 25 percent on all **merchandise.** This year, we will markdown only selected items. However, customers will be given coupons worth $10 each. They can use the coupons with any purchase over $100.

Paragraph 2

These are the procedures you should follow when ringing up purchases at the preholiday sale. First, ring up the full price of the item.

12   Chapter 2   Focusing Your Topic

Then deduct the markdown. When the entire purchase has been totaled, check whether or not it is over $100. If it is, subtract $10 for the coupon. Only one coupon can be used for each purchase.

1. What is the purpose of Paragraph 1?

   _____

2. What is the purpose of Paragraph 2?

   _____

3. How is information in Paragraph 1 different from the information in Paragraph 2?

   _____
   _____
   _____
   _____

Check your answers on page 130.

EXERCISE 1 Select Facts that Support Your Purpose

Below is a list of facts about the Peachtree Fashion Store that Mrs. Custis manages. Suppose Mrs. Custis was writing a letter to **managers** at the company's **headquarters,** asking permission to hire a new salesperson.

She wants the managers to know that sales and profits have increased. She wants them to realize that the workload in the store has also increased. Check the facts she should include.

_____ 1. Average number of dresses sold per month this year.

_____ 2. Increased sales and profits in recent months.

_____ 3. The success of a recent sale.

_____ 4. How many customers are in the store during peak hours.

_____ 5. Amount of commissions salespeople have earned recently.

_____ 6. The number of regular customers.

_____ 7. Rising profits over a three-year period.

_____ 8. The store's new, longer hours.

_____ 9. Reductions in the amount of unsold merchandise.

Check your answers on page 130.

Workplace Success 13

EXERCISE 2 Focus on Your Purpose

Use the points you checked in Exercise 1 to write a paragraph for Mrs. Custis. Remember that the purpose of your paragraph is to convince the managers to allow you to hire a new salesperson.

_____
_____
_____
_____
_____
_____
_____
_____
_____

Check your answers on page 130.

LESSON 2 Audience

It is important to keep your reader in mind as you write. Identifying your **audience** is a basic part of the prewriting stage. You would not, for example, write the same paragraph for your supervisor as you would for your best friend. Your attitude should be appropriate for your audience.

Another word for attitude is **tone.** Tone can be formal or informal, humorous or serious, friendly or cold. Your choice of words will help set your tone. To make your writing formal, avoid contractions and slang. To make your writing informal, you might address the reader as "you." When you reread what you write, pay attention to the tone your words create.

After you have decided who your audience is, you should think about these three questions:

1. How much does the audience know about the topic?
2. What does the audience care most about?
3. What attitude or tone is appropriate for this audience?

The answers to these questions will tell you what information to include in the paragraph and will help you state it in the right way.

EXAMPLE

Let's look at real-life examples of paragraphs addressed to two different audiences. Notice that the paragraphs are about the same topic, defective merchandise.

Paragraph 1

We are terribly sorry that the dress you bought at a Peachtree Fashion Store shrank when you washed it. We pride ourselves on carrying quality merchandise, and such **defects** are rare. We will give you a store **credit** for the full price of the purchase. In addition, please accept this **coupon** for $5 toward any future purchase you make at Peachtree Fashions. Thank you for letting us know about this problem.

Paragraph 2

Many of our customers have complained that dresses from your Splash-of-Spring line shrank in the wash even though they followed the **care instructions.** We have been buying merchandise from you for many years. This is the first time we have had a problem. I hope that you will take back the dresses our customers have returned to us as well as our unsold **stock.** I also hope that you will correct the problem that led to the defects in this line so that we can continue to buy from you.

1. Who is the audience for Example 1?

   _____

2. Who is the audience for Example 2?

   _____

3. How do the two paragraphs differ in tone?

   _____

   _____

Check your answers on page 130.

EXERCISE 1   Match the Information to the Audience

The following is a list of facts about a new shipment of dresses that Peachtree Fashion Stores received. Suppose you wanted to write to your regular customers about the dresses.

- Put an *M* next to the facts you would use with customers interested in saving *Money*.

- Put an *F* next to the facts that are best for customers who are interested in *Fashion*.

Workplace Success   15

- Put a *C* next to the facts that are good to use with customers who want *Comfort* and *Convenience*.

(Note that facts may be appropriate for more than one type of customer.)

_____ 1. The dresses were designed by one of the most popular designers.

_____ 2. The dresses are available in all sizes.

_____ 3. They are made from easy-care fabrics.

_____ 4. They are priced below wholesale.

_____ 5. They are the latest fashions.

_____ 6. They come in a range of designer colors.

_____ 7. They are appropriate for both day and evening.

_____ 8. They contain ten percent nylon for longer wear.

Check your answers on page 130.

EXERCISE 2 Write for Your Readers

Pick one type of customer from the following choices: most interested in saving money, most interested in fashion, or most interested in convenience. Write a paragraph using facts from Exercise 1 that would interest this customer in the new dresses.

_____
_____
_____
_____
_____
_____

Check your answers on page 130.

EXERCISE 3 Match Your Tone to Your Audience

Below is part of a letter Rosie wrote to a friend. Suppose Mrs. Custis asked Rosie to write a report about the same topic. Write a paragraph that Rosie could submit. Use facts from this letter to her friend.

Dear Meg,

Guess what? I'm a hero! I caught a shoplifter at the store today, and I impressed everybody, even Mrs. Custis. Here's what happened: I was watching Darlene make a sale to one of her "regulars" (for a change!) when this woman came into the store. When I went over to see if she needed help, she almost jumped out of her skin. She said, "No, no, no," in gulps. Anyway, I kept an eye on her. Sure enough, after wandering all over the place, looking at this and that, she slipped a necklace into her bag.

You'd be very proud of me, Meg. I really kept my cool. I walked quietly to Mrs. Custis and pointed the woman out. Mrs. Custis asked me to make sure that she didn't leave the store. Mrs. Custis went into the back to call the police. Meanwhile, I insisted on "helping" the customer. I talked to her and showed her merchandise. The police arrived fairly quickly, thank goodness!

When the shoplifter saw the police in the doorway, she went pale. She didn't make a bit of a fuss. After the police left with the woman, Mrs. Custis told me that she was proud of me.

Check your answers on page 130.

LESSON 3   Topic Sentence

A topic sentence summarizes the **main idea** of a paragraph. That is, it states the most important thing that you want to say about your topic. It sets the stage for what you plan to say in the rest of the paragraph. Your topic sentence helps you decide which information to include in your paragraph. The topic sentence is usually the first sentence. It helps readers understand the ideas and information in the rest of the paragraph.

Workplace Success

EXAMPLE

Look at a real-life example of a paragraph. Find the topic sentence.

> Starting October 15th, Peachtree Fashions will be open late two evenings a week. For the past six months, Peachtree Fashions has been open until 7 PM. on Thursdays. After October 15th, the store will remain open until 9 PM on Thursdays. In addition, Peachtree Fashions will remain open until 7 PM on Mondays. We hope these extended hours will make it more convenient for you to shop here. We look forward to seeing you on Monday and Thursday evenings. And of course, we also hope to see you during the day.

1. What is the topic of the paragraph?
   _____

2. What is the topic sentence of the paragraph?
   _____
   _____

3. What is the purpose of this paragraph?
   _____
   _____

Check your answers on page 130.

4. Who is the audience for the paragraph?
   _____
   _____

EXERCISE 1 Write a Topic Sentence

Read the following paragraph. Then write a topic sentence to begin the paragraph. Write the sentence on the lines provided.

_____
_____
_____

> Jennifer Kendra's first day will be October 15th, the day that our extended hours go into effect. She will work all day Saturday and Sunday, and on Monday and Thursday evenings. Jennifer has told me that she would also be happy to come in and help out during particularly busy times. I think this is good news for all of us on the regular sales staff. It means that we can put in less overtime and have less-hectic weekends and evenings. Please join me in welcoming Jennifer to the sales staff.

Check your answers on page 130.

EXERCISE 2 Identify and State the Topic Sentence

Reread the paragraph you wrote in Exercise 2 of Lesson 1 (page 14). Does it have a topic sentence? If so, copy the sentence below. If not, write a topic sentence you could add to the paragraph.

_____
_____

Check your answers on page 130.

EXERCISE 3 Put It All Together

Imagine that Mrs. Custis wants to send a notice to regular customers about a sale. In the notice, she wants to invite them to come to two special "preview" days. On these days, they can take advantage of the sale before it is announced to the public. Write the paragraph for Mrs. Custis. You can make up any details you want about the sale. Be sure to include a topic sentence in the paragraph.

_____
_____
_____
_____
_____
_____

Check your answers on page 130.

Workplace Success

FOR YOUR Portfolio

WRITE A PARAGRAPH TO REACH YOUR AUDIENCE AND ACHIEVE A PURPOSE

Some salespeople are paid a commission, a portion of each sale they make. This motivates them to sell as much as possible. Other salespeople are paid a **salary,** a fixed amount each week. A salary might be based on experience, quality of work, and cooperation, as well as sales.

Write a paragraph that gives your opinion about whether or not **retail** salespeople should get commissions. The purpose of the paragraph is either to persuade the management at Peachtree Fashion Stores to continue giving commissions or to stop giving commissions. Your audience is the managers at company headquarters. Be sure to include a topic sentence at the beginning of the paragraph.

_____
_____
_____
_____
_____
_____
_____
_____
_____
_____
_____
_____
_____
_____

CHAPTER 3

On the Job: Copy Center

Supporting Sentences

SOLVING **COMMUNICATION** PROBLEMS

Jamilla was doing some paperwork in the office of the copy shop when she heard someone shouting. She quickly put aside her work and went up front to see what was wrong. She found Mr. Horton, one of the Clear & Quick Copy Shop's best customers. He owned Horton's Restaurant two doors down the street. Every day, he brought in the list of specials to be photocopied. You could not ask for a better, more loyal customer. Now, however, Mr. Horton was angry.

"Blue paper!" he said, "I always have the specials copied on blue paper! Everybody knows that!"

Mei-Mei was the newest employee at Clear & Quick. She was close to tears as Mr. Horton raged.

"Can I do something for you, Mr. Horton?" Jamilla asked.

"You can throw away these copies," he said. "They are all wrong. My menu inserts have to be blue to go with the menu covers."

Mei-Mei pulled her shoulders back and grabbed the **order form.** "Look," she said, "Mr. Horton didn't say that he wanted blue paper."

Mr. Horton only got angrier. "You know, they just opened that fancy place down the block—Sha-Zam Service Center. I'm sure they would use blue paper. Not only that, they do it cheaper. The sign in their window says, 'Copies 7 cents.'"

Words at WORK

The following workplace terms are used in this chapter and are defined in the Glossary at the back of this book. If you do not know a word, first try to get the meaning by looking at it in context. Then consider any prefix, suffix, or root. If the meaning is still not clear, look it up in the Glossary.

chain
clustering
competition
desktop
discount
publishing
order form
promotion

APPLYING **COMMUNICATION** SKILLS

Write your answers to the following questions.

1. What is the main communication problem between Mei-Mei and Mr. Horton?

   _____
   _____
   _____

2. What might have caused it?

   _____
   _____
   _____
   _____

3. What are some possible solutions to the problem?

   _____
   _____
   _____
   _____
   _____
   _____

4. Select the one solution you think is best. Why would you suggest that Jamilla try it?

   _____
   _____
   _____
   _____
   _____
   _____

22   Chapter 3   Supporting Sentences

5. What do you think Jamilla should say to Mei-Mei after Mr. Horton leaves the store?

   _____
   _____
   _____
   _____
   _____

6. Can you think of a system for taking customers' orders that might lead to fewer errors? Write at least one idea on the following lines.

   _____
   _____
   _____
   _____
   _____

Check your answers on page 130.

LESSON 1 Brainstorming

To write a good paragraph you have to gather ideas. During the prewriting stage you collect as many ideas as you can without worrying about how you will use them. (You can weed out weaker ideas or ones that are off the topic later.) One way to gather ideas is by brainstorming. When you brainstorm you try to open your mind so that your ideas will flow. Your ideas can relate to your topic in any way at all. For example they may be:

- facts about the topic
- points you want to make about the topic
- things that happened to you or other people that relate to the topic
- reasons why your idea about the topic is a good one

When you brainstorm, you should write down all of your ideas without making judgments about them. If you can brainstorm with a partner or as part of a group, you may come up with more ideas. If you get stuck while brainstorming, try reading over the list of ideas you have so far to see if any of them inspires you.

Example:

Let's look at a real-life example of brainstorming.

> The Clear & Quick Copy Shop lost many customers to Sha-Zam, the brand-new service center down the block. Sha-Zam was part of a national **chain** and offered many services that Clear & Quick did not offer. Jamilla realized that she would have to do a better job of marketing in order to keep her customers. She asked everyone who worked at Clear & Quick to come up with ideas for new **promotions.** Below is the list Mei-Mei came up with when she brainstormed for ideas. Notice how wide-ranging Mei-Mei's ideas are. Think about which ones she might not have included if she had been making judgments about them.

Ideas for New Promotions

discount

coupons

ads

contests

serve coffee and donuts

neon sign for store

hand out fliers in front of Sha-Zam

give percent of profit to charity

membership cards for regular customers

T-shirts with logo on them

special prices for local businesses

get DJ to give a show from store

hold a party

sponsor a Little League team

Did you notice that Mei-Mei included some ideas that seem pretty silly on the surface, like holding a party or having a DJ give a show? When you brainstorm, write down *all* of your ideas, regardless of how outrageous they may seem.

24   Chapter 3   Supporting Sentences

EXERCISE 1 Jog Your Imagination

Check your answers on page 130.

Jamilla decided to run an ad in the local newspaper. She wanted her ad to be about the advantages of dealing with a small local shop over a large national chain. Brainstorm for ideas that Jamilla can include in the advertisement. Write your ideas on a separate sheet of paper.

EXERCISE 2 Brainstorm with Others

Check your answers on page 131.

Jamilla noticed that Sha-Zam sold merchandise in addition to offering copying, computer, and fax services. She asked her staff to get together and think about what merchandise they could sell in their small store. Get together with some of your friends, classmates, or family members and brainstorm for ideas. Write all the ideas on a separate sheet of paper.

LESSON 2 Clustering

Clustering is similar to brainstorming. In both you allow yourself to be as free as possible and use one idea to inspire another. With **clustering**, however, you organize these ideas into a visual pattern. Begin by writing the topic, or a key word related to the topic, in the center of a blank page. Circle the word. Around it, write other ideas the topic brings to mind. Circle these ideas, and draw arrows from the topic to them. Now you use each of these ideas as a starting point for coming up with more ideas. In this way, you can work further and further out from the center, coming up with clusters of related ideas. Sometimes clustering is called **mapping**.

EXAMPLE

Let's look at a real-life example of clustering.

Jamilla decided that she needed to expand the services she offered at Clear & Quick. She used clustering to come up with ideas for services. Her clustering resulted in the diagram that follows. When you look at the cluster diagram, pay attention to the way ideas are related to each other.

Workplace Success   25

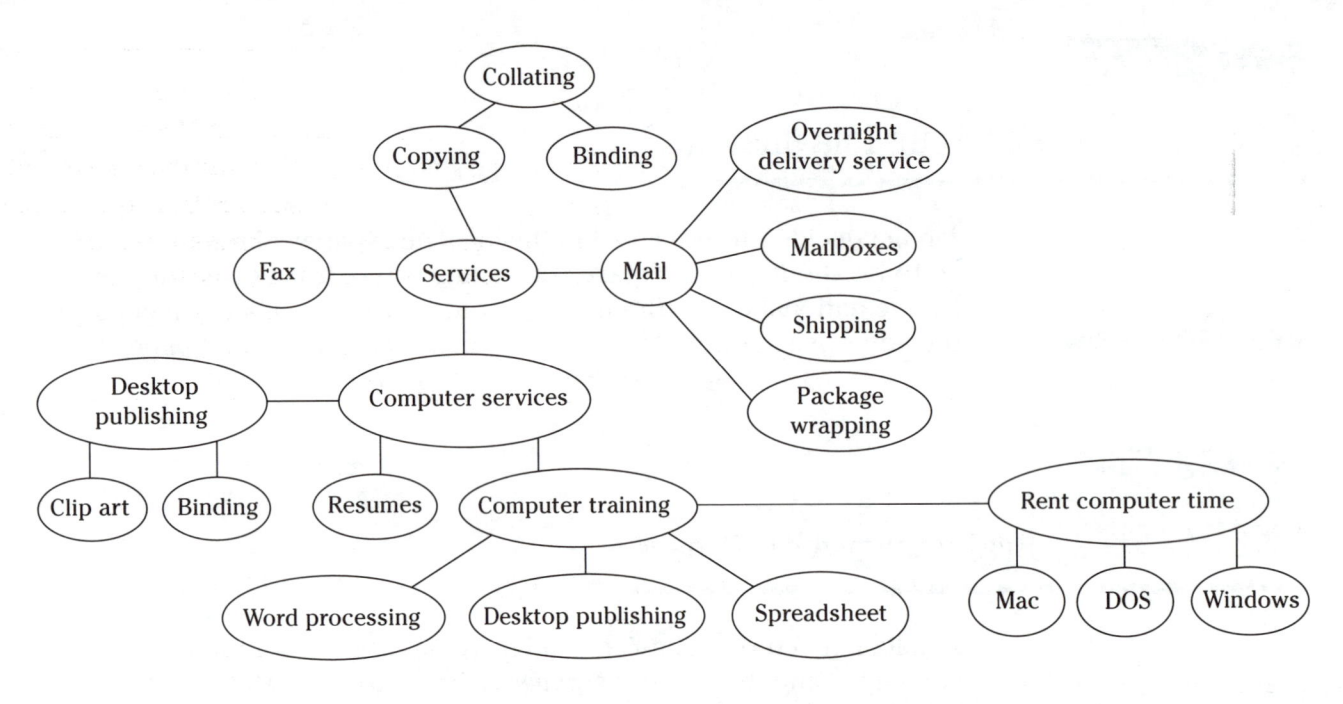

```
                    Collating
              Copying    Binding    Overnight
                                   delivery service
                                        Mailboxes
        Fax   Services   Mail
                                        Shipping
  Desktop     Computer services         Package
  publishing                            wrapping

Clip art  Binding  Resumes  Computer training ─────── Rent computer time

          Word processing  Desktop publishing  Spreadsheet    Mac  DOS  Windows
```

1. What idea did *computer training* grow out of?

   _____

   _____

Check your
answers on
page 131.

2. What ideas grew out of *computer training*?

   _____

   _____

EXERCISE 1 Develop New Ideas

Check your answers
on page 131.

Jamilla realized that dealing with a copy shop is not always pleasant for customers. She wants ideas about how to make using Clear & Quick Copy Shop a more pleasant experience. Use clustering to come up with ideas for Jamilla. If you are unfamiliar with copy shops, cluster ideas about how to make shopping in another kind of store more pleasant. Use a separate sheet of paper.

EXERCISE 2 Plan a Promotion

Check your answers
on page 131.

Pick one of the promotion ideas from Mei-Mei's brainstorming list on page 24. Cluster to develop some ideas for how Clear & Quick could use this form of promotion.

LESSON 3 Organizing Ideas

Once you have gathered as many ideas as possible for a paragraph, it is time to organize them. The first step in organizing ideas is to weed out the ones that you will not use. The ideas you include (or keep) should be the right ones for both your audience and your purpose for writing.

To organize the ideas you have kept, look at how they are related. Group ideas together that are related to the same **subtopic.**

The final step in organizing your ideas is to decide in what order they will fall within the paragraph. There are a number of possible ways to order your ideas. Five of the most common are sequential order, chronological order, spatial order, order of importance, and comparison and contrast.

- *Sequential Order.* In **sequential order,** the supporting details are arranged according to the way they logically come after one another. Alphabetical order and numerical order are both forms of sequential order. When you list items by size, from smallest to largest (or vice versa), you are using sequential order.

- *Chronological Order.* In **chronological order,** the supporting details are arranged according to when they happened or will happen. Chronological order is most often used in **narrative writing** (writing that tells a story) or in writing that tells how something is done. Chronological order is a form of sequential order.

- *Spatial Order.* In **spatial order,** you relate ideas according to their position in space. For example, a paragraph arranged in spatial order might move from top to bottom or left to right. Spatial order is most often used in **descriptions.** Spatial order is also a form of sequential order.

- *Order of Importance.* You can also rank the ideas according to how important they are. You can either go from most important to least important or from least important to most important. **Order of importance** is most often used in paragraphs that state opinions or aim to persuade readers to think or do something.

- *Comparison and Contrast.* You can use **comparison and contrast** to organize information that tells about how two things are alike and different. One way to use comparison and contrast is to first describe all of the characteristics of one item then describe the same characteristics of the other item. Another was is to alternate between the two items, writing about one characteristic at a time.

EXAMPLE

Let's look at the real-life example of the list of promotion ideas Mei-Mei came up with. Notice how she crossed out the ideas that she did not think were good and numbered the remaining ideas to change their order.

Workplace Success 27

(1) discount

(2) coupons

(3) ads

(6) contests

(7) serve coffee and donuts

~~neon sign for store~~

(4) hand out fliers in front of Sha-Zam

~~give percent of profit to charity~~

~~membership cards for regular customers~~

~~T-shirts with a logo on them~~

~~special prices for local businesses~~

~~get DJ to give a show from store~~

(5) hold a party

~~sponsor a Little League team~~

1. What do ideas 1 and 2 have in common?

    _____

2. What do ideas 3 and 4 have in common?

    _____

Check your answers on page 131.

3. What do ideas 5, 6, and 7 have in common?

    _____

EXERCISE 1 Decide on the Right Order

Decide which method of organization would be best for a paragraph on each of the following topics. Choose from the following: sequential, chronological, spatial, order of importance, or comparison and contrast. Write your choice on the lines provided.

1. Services available at Sha-Zam and services available at Clear & Quick.

    _____

2. Procedures for taking an order from a customer at Clear & Quick.

    _____

28   Chapter 3   Supporting Sentences

3. Instructions for using the new binding machine that Clear & Quick just installed.

   _____

4. Description of Sha-Zam's new shop.

   _____

5. Reasons for running a newspaper ad for Clear & Quick.

   _____

6. A job description for a clerk at Clear & Quick.

   _____

7. An announcement telling about new services at Clear & Quick.

   _____

8. The quantities of the different color papers in stock at Clear & Quick.

   _____

Check your answers on page 131.

EXERCISE 2 Group Your Ideas

Think about the ad Jamilla wants to write about the advantages of using a small shop like Clear & Quick. Choose the ideas from your brainstorming list from Exercise 1 of Lesson 1 (page 25) that you want to include in the paragraph. Write those ideas on the lines below. Review your new list to see how the ideas are related to each other. Use lines to connect ideas that go together.

_____	_____
_____	_____
_____	_____
_____	_____
_____	_____
_____	_____

Check your answers on page 131.

Workplace Success 29

EXERCISE 3 Put Your Ideas in Order

Review your list in Exercise 2. Think about the topic of your paragraph, your purpose for writing it, and your audience (Jamilla, your employer at Clear & Quick). Decide what method of organization you will use for the paragraph. Then rewrite your list of ideas in the order in which you will use them in the paragraph.

_____   _____

_____   _____

_____   _____

_____   _____

Check your answers on page 131.

FYI

ORGANIZING WITH AN OUTLINE

When organizing ideas for a paragraph, you will probably only need to number them or write them in order. For a longer piece of writing, however, you may need to make an outline that shows how all the topics and subtopics are related. This outline is for a report based on the ideas Jamilla thought of to beat the competition. Notice how she used Roman numerals for the topics, and capital letters, Arabic numerals, and lowercase letters for the subtopics.

I. Promotion Campaign
    A. Advertising
        1. Newspaper
        2. Fliers
    B. Discounts and Coupons

II. New Merchandise
    A. School and office supplies
    B. Greeting cards and gift wrapping

III. New services
    A. Computer Services
        1. Computer Training
        2. Computer Time
    B. Mail
        1. Overnight delivery
        2. Mailboxes
    C. Desktop publishing
        1. Binding
        2. Clip Art

IV. Fax

FOR YOUR Portfolio

GATHER AND ORGANIZE IDEAS FOR A PARAGRAPH

You are going to write a paragraph about alternatives to having customers fill out their own order forms. Before you start, spend some time coming up with ideas and organizing them. First, use your answer to question 6 on page 23 to spark your imagination. Then brainstorm for more ideas. Write these ideas here.

_____

_____

_____

_____

_____

_____

_____

_____

_____

_____

_____

_____

_____

_____

_____

Next, look through your brainstorming ideas and decide which ones you want to use in your paragraph. Cross out the ideas you are not going to use. Copy the ideas that you will use onto a separate sheet of paper. Group them according to subtopic.

Think about the purpose of the paragraph to decide what method of organization you will use. Once you have selected the form of organization, number your ideas to show the order they will appear in the paragraph. Finally, write your paragraph on a separate sheet of paper.

Workplace Success

CHAPTER 4

Concluding Sentence

On the Job: Copy Center

SOLVING COMMUNICATION PROBLEMS

Jamilla felt wonderful. What a great day! It had been a year since the Sha-Zam Service Center had opened down the block, and here she was still in business, still earning a profit. She even had to take on a new staff member. That morning, Jamilla had asked Mr. Horton to bring donuts along with the urn of coffee he delivered every day now. She invited the staff to celebrate by sharing Mr. Horton's fine baked goods. While they ate, she "toasted" them with her coffee, praising them for their efforts over the past year.

Jamilla smiled as she asked Mei-Mei to stand next to her, and handed her the beautiful blue coffee mug.

"I'm giving Mei-Mei a special award for coming up with the cleverest idea," Jamilla said. "Who would have thought that free coffee would be a key to our survival? Think of all of those impatient customers down the block, grumbling while they're waiting for their copies. Our customers, on the other hand, sit comfortably on the bench out front while they drink fresh-brewed coffee."

Later, Jamilla overheard Mei-Mei talking to Bradley, one of the new clerks.

"Can you believe it?" Mei-Mei asked, "I get this cheap coffee mug, when I just about saved the business? If she thinks she can buy my loyalty with a mug, she's got to be crazy. Remember that meeting when she asked for our ideas? She said that the person who came up with the best idea would get a **bonus.** Some bonus! Even if my mug is filled with free coffee for the rest of my life, it's hardly worth it."

Words at WORK

The following workplace terms are used in this chapter and are defined in the Glossary at the back of this book. If you do not know a word, first try to get the meaning by looking at it in context. Then consider any prefix, suffix, or root. If the meaning is still not clear, look it up in the Glossary.

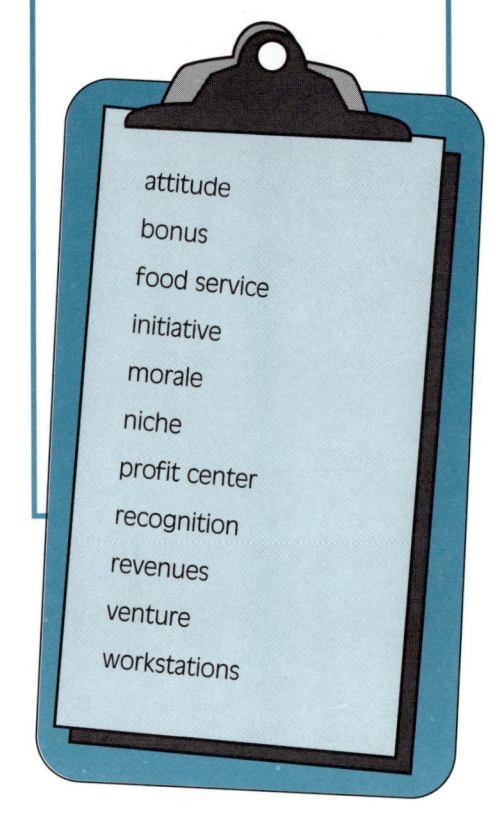

- attitude
- bonus
- food service
- initiative
- morale
- niche
- profit center
- recognition
- revenues
- venture
- workstations

Jamilla's good mood was shattered. She felt terrible. Had she really said that she'd give a bonus? She couldn't remember. Clearly, however, a bonus would have been in order. What could she do now? She didn't want Mei-Mei to feel bad. More importantly, she didn't want Mei-Mei lowering the **morale,** or spirit, of the staff by sharing her disappointment with them.

APPLYING **COMMUNICATION** SKILLS

Write your answers to the following questions.

1. What is the main communication problem between Jamilla and Mei-Mei?

   _____
   _____

2. What might have caused it?

   _____
   _____

3. What are some possible solutions to the problem?

   _____
   _____
   _____
   _____
   _____
   _____

4. Select the one solution that you think is best. Why would you suggest that Jamilla try it?

   _____
   _____
   _____
   _____

5. What kind of rewards can employers offer employees to let them know that they're appreciated? Do such rewards help build staff morale? Write down your ideas about this subject.

Check your answers on page 131.

LESSON 1   Content and Placement of a Concluding Sentence

You have identified the audience for your paragraph, defined your purpose, selected a topic, and gathered and organized your ideas. You may think you are now ready to leave the prewriting stage of the writing process. But you are not quite finished yet. Most paragraphs need one last thing to tie them together, a conclusion.

As its name suggests, a **concluding sentence** of a paragraph is usually a single sentence. However, some paragraphs may require more than one concluding sentence. The conclusion is usually placed at the very end of the paragraph. It summarizes the major points you made.

EXAMPLE

Let's look at a real-life example of a pair of concluding sentences. They are from a paragraph that Mei-Mei wrote when she got an even bigger idea. First look at the concluding sentences by themselves. They contain the most important ideas from the paragraph. Therefore, you should be able to figure out what Mei-Mei said in the rest of the paragraph.

... The new coffee bar will be a way to build business and increase **revenues.** *It will also keep up with the latest retailing trend.*

1. What do you think the topic of the paragraph is?

2. What points do you think Mei-Mei makes in her paragraph?

Check your answers on page 131.

34   Chapter 4   Concluding Sentence

Now read the entire paragraph to learn how much you found out about it from the concluding sentences.

> We should think about adding a coffee bar to the copy shop. With the store between Clear & Quick and Horton's Restaurant empty, this is the perfect moment to do it. Mr. Horton can join in the **venture** by running the **food service** operation. We now know that our customers enjoy relaxing over a cup of coffee while they wait for their copies. Think of how much more enjoyment they will get when they can have a muffin, or one of Mr. Horton's delicious donuts. In addition, a promotion that is now costing us money can be turned into a **profit center** for Clear & Quick and for Mr. Horton.

EXERCISE 1 Find the Concluding Sentence

Look for the sentence or sentences in each paragraph that states the conclusion. Copy the concluding sentence(s) on the lines following the paragraphs.

1. We are sorry we cannot always handle your orders instantly. We know you hate to wait—who doesn't? Unfortunately, no one has yet come up with a way to take care of everybody at once. So, despite the efforts of our dedicated staff, it may take a few minutes to get your job done. We want to make your time at Clear & Quick as pleasant as possible. Therefore, we would like you to help yourself to a free cup of coffee while you wait. Feel free to sit on one of the benches out front while you drink it.

   _____

   _____

2. Everybody who works at Clear & Quick is special. (Otherwise, I would not have hired you!) Sometimes, however, staff members do something above and beyond the call of duty. You might have put in extra time to get out a rush job. You might have helped a customer solve a tricky problem, such as finding a way to bind an oversized report. Or you might have come up with a way to do your job more efficiently. Whatever it is, special efforts deserve **recognition.** So from now on, I am going to honor one outstanding employee every month.

   _____

   _____

3. Mei-Mei Han has been named Employee of the Month for October. Over the past year, Mei-Mei has come up with a number of good ideas to help us compete with Sha-Zam. Her idea for serving coffee, for example, has been a big success. Now she has developed a larger concept—a coffee bar. Clearly, Mei-Mei is making an extra effort to help Clear & Quick succeed. Her picture will be posted under the "Employee of the Month" banner until November 1.

_____

_____

_____

_____

Check your answers on page 131.

EXERCISE 2 Choose the Correct Concluding Sentence

Read each of the following paragraphs. Then select the concluding sentence(s) that best fits the paragraph. Put a check mark next to your choice.

1. The Sha-Zam Service Center is at least three times as large as Clear & Quick's. It is run by a national chain. The chain gives advertising and promotional support. Sha-Zam offers many business services in addition to photocopying. It offers six computer **workstations,** desktop publishing, and other computer services for customers. The copying machines are the latest models. Clear & Quick, on the other hand, does not have space or money to offer all of these services. We do, however, have the ability to do a full range of copying jobs quickly and efficiently.

   _____ a. Space at Clear & Quick is limited. Therefore, we are unable to compete against Sha-Zam.

   _____ b. There is no point in trying to compete with Sha-Zam on all services. Instead, Clear & Quick should find it's own **niche,** or special place, in the market.

   _____ c. Clear & Quick should put in an equal number of computer workstations to Sha-Zam's.

2. Starting on September 1, you will receive a five percent pay raise. You have been with us a year now, Mei-Mei, and during that time, you have learned a great deal. You work hard, and our customers are always pleased by your pleasant **attitude.** Not only that, you have shown **initiative.** You have taken action to give Clear & Quick

36   Chapter 4   Concluding Sentence

the benefit of your excellent ideas. I'm particularly pleased with the way you responded after Sha-Zam opened up last fall. Your idea for offering coffee was a great help.

_____ a. Clearly, you deserve this raise, and I'm very happy that you're a member of our team.

_____ b. All employees will be getting five percent raises this year.

_____ c. You should, however, be more careful to make sure that you take customers' orders correctly.

Check your answers on page 131.

EXERCISE 3 Sum It Up

Below is a paragraph from a letter that Jamilla wrote to Mr. Horton. Help Jamilla strengthen her case by adding a concluding sentence to the paragraph. Write your concluding sentence on the line below the paragraph.

> I think the coffee bar would be good for both our businesses. I am sure you have noticed, as I have, how busy the coffee bar on the corner of Webster Street is. (In fact, you may have lost some business to it.) The coffee bar would be a way for you to attract new customers. People who now drink your coffee at Clear & Quick would be likely to go to the coffee bar. Not only will they have a cup of coffee, but they might also buy something to eat with it. Once they have tasted your delicious pastries, they are likely come back, even when they do not need any photocopies. Indeed, they may go on to try your restaurant for a full meal.

Check your answers on page 131.

EXERCISE 4 Write a Paragraph with a Concluding Sentence

Check your answers on page 131.

Turn back to Exercise 3 in Lesson 3 of Chapter 3 (page 30). There you organized ideas for a paragraph about kinds of merchandise Clear & Quick might sell. Draft the paragraph on a separate sheet of paper. Be sure to include a concluding sentence.

Workplace Success   37

LESSON 2   Unity

The topic sentence, supporting sentences, and concluding sentences should all work together to give your readers the information you want them to have. When this is the case, the paragraph has **unity**. In a unified paragraph, all the information relates to the topic and main idea. You can make sure your paragraphs have unity by following these steps:

1. Identify the topic and main idea of the paragraph.
2. Think about each supporting detail, one at a time. Ask yourself whether or not it relates to the topic and main idea.
3. If a detail does not relate to the topic and main idea, eliminate it.
4. Think about the concluding sentence. Ask yourself if it clearly relates to the topic and main idea.
5. If the concluding sentence does not clearly relate to the topic and main idea, restate it to make the relationship clear.

Example:

Let's look at a real-life example of a paragraph with unity. As you read the paragraph, look for the topic and main idea. Then think about how each sentences relates to the main idea.

ANNOUNCEMENT

Horton's Restaurant and Clear & Quick Copy Shop are pleased to announce the opening of Horton's Rich & Quick Coffee Bar. Located at 75 Merchant Street, Rich & Quick is jointly owned by Horton's and Clear & Quick. It serves a full range of coffees and light snacks. It is open daily from 10 AM to 6 PM. Please drop in for a cup of delicious coffee in comfortable and friendly surroundings.

Did you see that the topic of the paragraph is Horton's Rich & Quick Coffee Bar? Did you notice that the main idea is that Horton's Restaurant and Clear and Quick Copy Shop have opened a coffee bar? The paragraph has unity because every sentence tells you something about the new coffee bar.

EXERCISE 1   Recognize Details that Do Not Belong

Decide which details *do not* belong in the following paragraph. Write the numbers of the sentences that contain these details below the paragraph. (Hint: find the topic sentence first.)

(1) The coffee bar might carry some items in addition to pastries. (2) Sandwiches and salads would bring in customers who would like a light lunch. (3) Horton's Restaurant sells a wider range of sandwiches than the coffee bar would. (4) The restaurant also sells hot meals. (5) Fresh fruit and yogurt would appeal to the healthy eater. (6) The coffee bar could also sell pretzels, chips, and other snack foods. (7) If we offer ice cream and soft drinks, we will attract families with children.

Check your answers on page 131.

EXERCISE 2 Select Details that Belong

The following list includes ideas for Horton's Rich & Quick Coffee Bar. Choose details that relate only to the physical appearance of the bar. Put check marks next to your choices.

_____ 1. Old movie posters on the walls.

_____ 2. Red and white striped shirts and black slacks for counter people.

_____ 3. Long wooden counter with coffee urns and espresso machine.

_____ 4. Red trays and white napkins with "Rich & Quick" printed in red.

_____ 5. Four kinds of sandwiches every day.

_____ 6. One vegetarian salad every day.

_____ 7. A glass display case for pastries.

_____ 8. Coffee in three sizes, small ($0.75), medium ($1.25), and large ($1.75).

Check your answers on page 131.

EXERCISE 3 Write a Unified Paragraph

Write a paragraph about the physical appearance of Horton's Rich & Quick. Start by determining the main idea. Then write a topic sentence. Use details from Exercise 2 in the supporting sentences. End with a concluding sentence that ties together the information in the paragraph. Give the paragraph unity by including only information and ideas that relate to the topic and main idea. Use a separate sheet of paper.

Check your answers on page 132.

Workplace Success   39

FOR YOUR Portfolio

WRITE A PARAGRAPH WITH A STRONG CONCLUSION

Write a paragraph about ways of rewarding employees for doing excellent work. Your audience for the paragraph is owners of small businesses, such as Jamilla. Before you write the paragraph, first brainstorm or cluster your ideas on separate paper. Then organize your ideas. Finally, write your paragraph on the lines below. Be sure the paragraph includes a topic sentence and ends with a strong concluding sentence.

CHAPTER 5

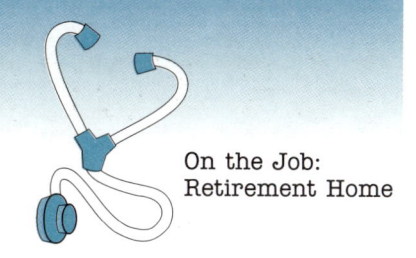

On the Job: Retirement Home

Kinds of Paragraphs: Informative, Descriptive, Narrative

SOLVING **COMMUNICATION** PROBLEMS

It was time for Mr. Demasi's **physical therapy** session at Sunset House, the **retirement home** where he lives. However, Kevin Duane, his aide, couldn't find him. After checking his room and the lounge, Kevin asked his supervisor, Alberto Torres, what to do. Alberto was especially worried because Mr. Demasi had severe **hypertension.** Alberto had just decided to ask Susan Long, the staff **social worker,** when Mr. Demasi and his nephew walked in. Alberto raced over to them.

"Thank goodness!" he exclaimed. "Where have you been?"

Mr. Demasi's nephew looked puzzled. "It's such a nice day," he said, "we thought we'd go out for a drive."

"You should have checked out first," Alberto told him.

"Why?" asked the nephew. "Uncle Ralph isn't a prisoner."

"He's already missed half his physical therapy session," Alberto explained.

"I think on a day like today, a little fresh air is what my uncle needs."

"Suppose it had been time for his **medication?**" Alberto continued. "It could be dangerous to miss it."

The nephew turned to his uncle and said, "Uncle Ralph, was it time for your medication?"

Mr. Demasi replied, "No, I take it with breakfast."

"See what I mean? My uncle knows what he's doing, and I don't think you have any right to control his life this way."

Words at **WORK**

The following workplace terms are used in this chapter and are defined in the Glossary at the back of this book. If you do not know a word, first try to get the meaning by looking at it in context. Then consider any prefix, suffix, or root. If the meaning is still not clear, look it up in the Glossary.

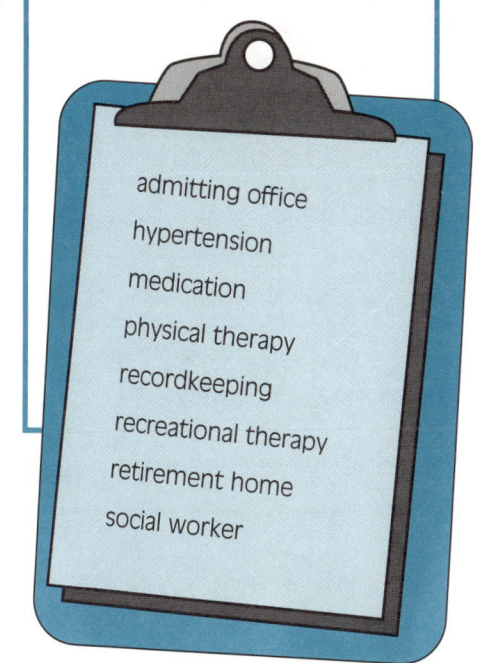

admitting office
hypertension
medication
physical therapy
recordkeeping
recreational therapy
retirement home
social worker

APPLYING COMMUNICATION SKILLS

Write your answers to the following questions.

1. What is the main communication problem between Alberto and Mr. Demasi's nephew?

   _____
   _____
   _____

2. What might have caused it?

   _____
   _____
   _____
   _____

3. What are some possible solutions to the problem?

   _____
   _____
   _____
   _____
   _____
   _____

4. Select the one solution you think is best. What would you suggest that Alberto try?

   _____
   _____
   _____

5. How might written guidelines for residents and their families help avoid these misunderstandings?

   _____
   _____
   _____

6. What are some items you think should be included in such guidelines?

_____

_____

_____

_____

_____

_____

_____

Check your answers on page 132.

LESSON 1 Paragraphs that Inform

Whatever your job, you will probably need to follow instructions that explain how to do something. You may also have to write down instructions for other people to follow.

To plan a paragraph that explains how to do something, ask yourself the following three questions:

1. *What do I want to explain?* The answer to this question will tell you the topic of your paragraph.

2. *What steps are needed to do this activity?* To answer this question, go through the steps yourself, taking notes about what you do.

3. *Who is my audience?* Knowing the answer will help you decide what information to include and if you need to define some terms.

You can use the answers to these questions to draft your paragraph. Turn the answer to Question 1 above into a topic sentence for the paragraph. The steps that you identified for Question 2 above will become the other sentences in the paragraph. Give the steps in **chronological order,** that is the order in which they happen in time. Or you may give the steps in **sequential order,** which is step-by-step. Using signal words, such as *first, then,* and *finally,* will help readers follow the order. Keep in mind the answer to Question 3 as you write so you will know how much detail to include.

SIGNAL WORDS FOR CHRONOLOGICAL OR SEQUENTIAL ORDER

first	then	before	to start
second	next	after	finally
third	while	during	in conclusion

Workplace Success   43

EXAMPLE

Let's look at a real-life example of a paragraph that explains to aides at Sunset House how to do part of their job.

> You should try to make new residents' first impression of Sunset House a good one. To start, greet the resident and family members warmly and introduce yourself when they first arrive. All new residents must stop at the **admitting office** before they go to their rooms. Take the resident and family members there, and wait for them while they are interviewed by a member of the staff. Residents will also be given several forms that they or a family member must complete. Offer the resident any physical assistance needed for this task. After the resident is finished, take him or her (and the family) to the resident's room. Allow the family time alone to settle in. But tell them when you will be back to give them a tour of Sunset House. All new residents must see the staff **social worker** and doctor. Tell the resident the times his or her appointments are scheduled for, and offer to act as a guide.

1. What is the topic of the paragraph? What is the topic sentence?

   _____

   _____

2. How are the steps arranged?

   _____

Check your answers on page 132.

3. Underline the signal words in the paragraph that help readers to follow these steps. Then write these words in the following space.

   _____

   _____

EXERCISE 1 Put the Steps in Order

Suppose a new resident decides to go alone to the first meeting with the social worker. The resident asks you how to get to the social worker's office. The following list gives the route that the resident needs to follow. The steps are not given in the proper order or sequence. Number the steps to show the correct order. Use the floor plan as a guide.

44 Chapter 5 Kinds of Paragraphs: Informative, Descriptive, Narrative

Sunset House Ground Floor

Old Building

a. _____ right at the stairwell.

b. _____ left at the end of the corridor.

c. _____ door at the end of corridor.

d. _____ through the door to the new wing.

e. _____ to the end of the corridor.

Check your answers on page 132.

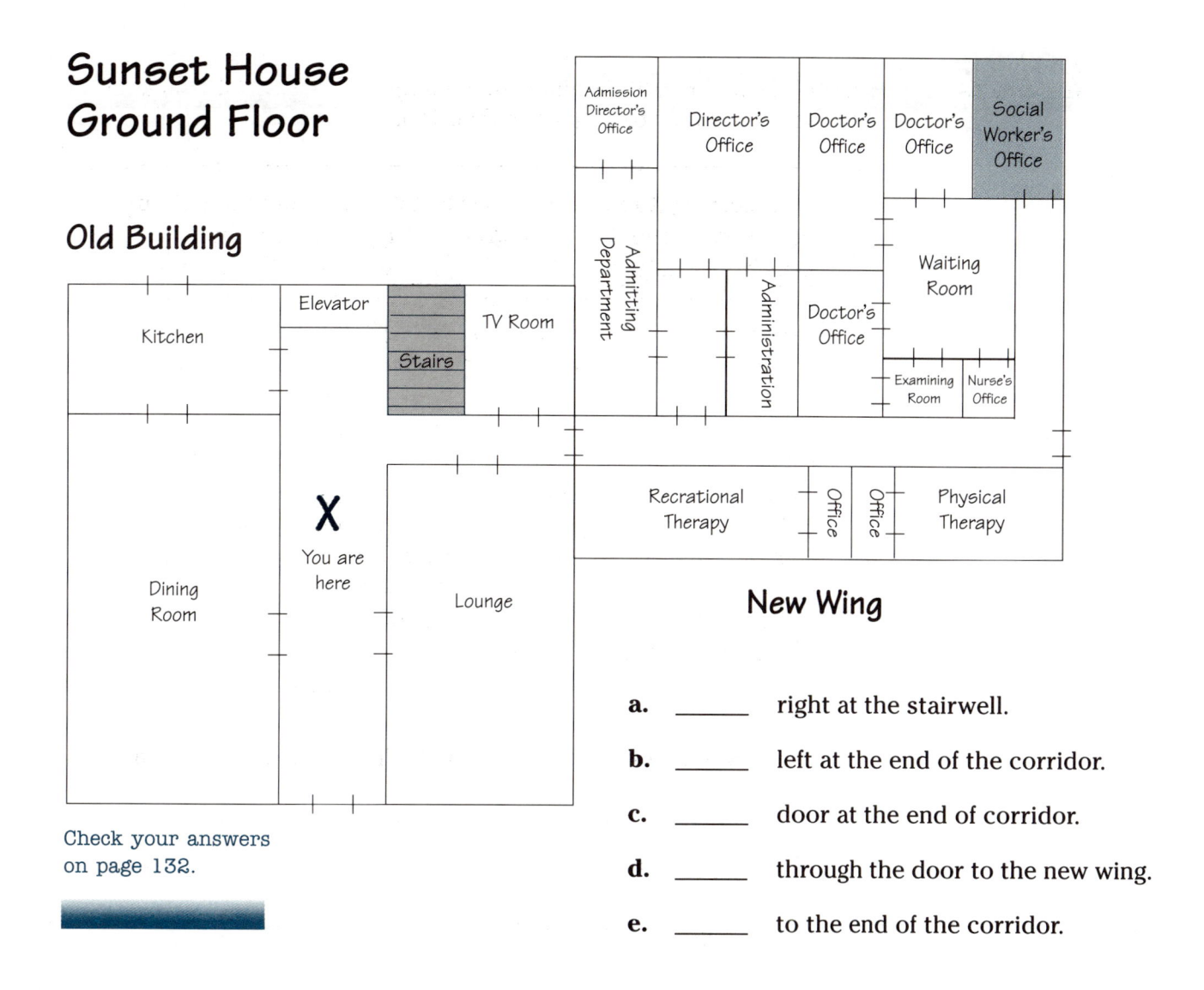

EXERCISE 2 Tell How It's Done

First write a topic sentence for a paragraph that explains how to direct new residents to the social worker's office from the elevator or stairs. Then complete the paragraph, using the steps in Exercise 1 as a guide. Add signal words to help readers follow your explanation.

_____
_____
_____
_____
_____
_____

Check your answers on page 132.

Workplace Success   45

LESSON 2 Paragraphs that Describe

Descriptive paragraphs tell what something or someone is like. Descriptive paragraphs help readers see, feel, taste, smell, and hear the thing being described. The topic sentence gives the overall impression. Supporting sentences include specific details about the person, place, or thing being described.

When you write a descriptive paragraph, try to use specific words, action verbs, and vivid details. You can write a descriptive paragraph by following these steps.

1. Observe or recall the subject of your paragraph carefully. Note sensory details; that is, the things you can see, feel, taste, smell, and hear.

2. Write a topic sentence that gives your overall impression of the subject.

3. Write supporting sentences that contain vivid details. You do not need to include every detail you observed or recalled. Rather, pick the ones that will most help the reader get the sense of what the subject is like.

EXAMPLE

Look at two paragraphs that describe Sunset House.

a. Sunset House is located in a brick mansion on a quiet country estate. The 50 private rooms are decorated with comfortable furniture. The dining hall, lounge, and TV room give residents ample opportunity to spend time together. A modern wing has been added. It contains state-of-the-art medical facilities and facilities for physical and **recreational therapy.**

b. Sunset House is located in a country house. It has 50 private rooms for residents, a common dining hall, lounge, and TV room. It also has facilities for medical care, and physical and recreational therapy.

1. Which paragraph would you want to use in a brochure about the center?

    _____

2. Which details in the paragraph you chose helped you picture Sunset House?

    _____
    _____
    _____
    _____

Check your answers on page 132.

46   Chapter 5   Kinds of Paragraphs: Informative, Descriptive, Narrative

EXERCISE 1 Choose Specific Words

Each of the words below is a general word. Write five specific words that could replace the general word. You may use a dictionary or thesaurus to get started. The first one has been done for you.

1. walk: _saunter, pace, stagger, limp, tread_

2. speak: _____

3. building: _____

4. dog: _____

5. person: _____

6. shoes: _____

7. go: _____

8. like: _____

Check your answers on page 132.

EXERCISE 2 Paint Pictures with Words

For each pair of sentences, pick the sentence that paints a more vivid picture. Circle the letter of the sentence.

1a. Aides distributed snacks to the residents this afternoon.

1b. Aides distributed juice and cookies to the residents this afternoon.

2a. Kevin noted that Mr. Hendrix was more cheerful this morning, and his color was better.

2b. Kevin noted that Mr. Hendrix seemed healthier this morning.

3a. Sunset House serves good food.

3b. The food at Sunset House is both wholesome and tasty.

4a. The aides take disabled residents to recreational therapy. There the residents enjoy weaving, pottery, jewelry making, painting, and other arts and crafts.

4b. The aides take disabled residents to recreational therapy, where the residents make different things.

Check your answers on page 132.

Workplace Success

EXERCISE 3 Describe a Place

Study the picture of the lounge at Sunset House. Then write a paragraph that describes the lounge. Use a separate sheet of paper.

Check your answers on page 132.

48   Chapter 5   Kinds of Paragraphs: Informative, Descriptive, Narrative

LESSON 3   Narrative Paragraphs

Narrative paragraphs are paragraphs that tell about something that happened. Such paragraphs are used in stories, novels, and newspapers. You may be surprised to learn that they are also used at work. When you write narrative paragraphs at work, they usually include only facts, rather than opinions or made-up stories.

Narrative paragraphs answer the following questions: Who was involved? What happened? Where did it happen? When did it happen? They often also tell why and how the events happened. Narrative paragraphs are usually arranged in chronological order.

EXAMPLE

Look at an example of a narrative paragraph that a physical therapist wrote about Mrs. Wong's progress in physical therapy.

When Mrs. Wong arrived at Sunset House last October, I observed that she was too weak to walk more than a few steps, and she spent most of her time in a wheelchair. I started her on a course of physical therapy that included massage and exercise. Gradually, Mrs. Wong's strength increased. After three months of therapy, she is now able to use a walker for an hour a day.

1. Who was involved?

   _____

2. What happened?

   _____
   _____

3. Where did it happen?

   _____

4. When did it happen?

   _____

5. How did it happen?

   _____
   _____

Check your answers on page 132.

EXERCISE 1 Tell What Happened

Look at the pictures carefully to find out about an accident at Sunset House. Then write a narrative paragraph that tells what happened. Use a separate sheet of paper.

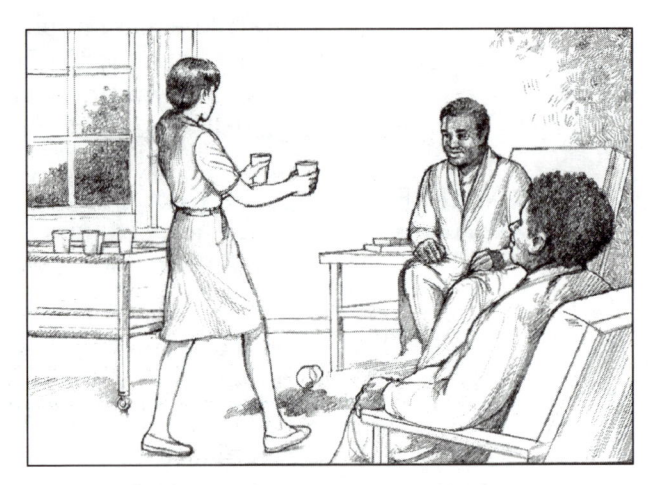

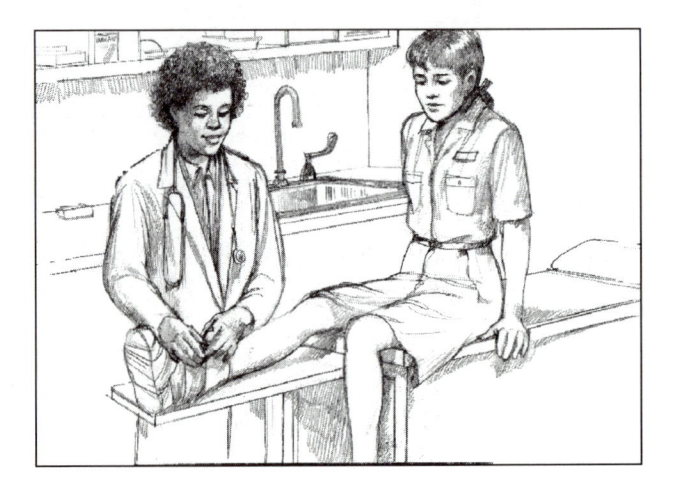

Check your answers on page 132.

50   Chapter 5   Kinds of Paragraphs: Informative, Descriptive, Narrative

FOR YOUR Portfolio

WRITE THREE KINDS OF PARAGRAPHS

1. Come up with five procedures that patients leaving the grounds of the center have to follow. (Reread Solving Communications Problems on page 41.) Then write an informative paragraph for the relatives of residents explaining these procedures.

2. Now, imagine that Mr. Demasi has not returned, and you have to write a report about the incident. First write a narrative paragraph that tells what happened. Then write a descriptive paragraph that tells what Mr. Demasi looks like. It should be possible for the police to use the second paragraph to search for Mr. Demasi. Use your imagination to fill in information about his appearance. Begin writing below, and continue on a separate sheet of paper.

Workplace Success

CHAPTER 6

On the Job: Retirement Home

Kinds of Paragraphs: Persuasive

SOLVING **COMMUNICATION** PROBLEMS

"I'm sure I ordered item D-37295, not item D-237296," Melanie told Herman Broadman. "After all, that's what I always order."

Herman is a customer service representative at Ace Medical Equipment, Sunset House's main **supplier.** Last week Melanie Chan, a clerk at Sunset House, placed a telephone order for a **gross** of thermometers. When the order arrived, she found that all the thermometers measured temperature in **Celsius,** rather than **Fahrenheit**. She called Herman to have the problem corrected. She was trying to stay calm, but she hated talking to Herman about problems.

Herman was reliable and usually very helpful, but he tended to be cranky when things went wrong. Now he told Melanie, "Look, I remember writing up the order and wondering why you wanted Celsius. Check your **purchase order.** What does it say?'"

"You know I don't have a purchase order," Melanie reminded Herman. "I *called* in the order."

"That's right," Herman told her. "That's when I asked why you wanted Celsius thermometers." Melanie knew he had never asked this question; but it didn't matter. The important thing now was to fix the situation.

"However it happened, Herman," she now told him, "we now have 144 Celsius thermometers that we can't use. I'd like to send them back and have you ship Fahrenheit thermometers."

"Sure, Melanie," Herman said, "I'd be happy to send them, but you're going to have to pay shipping costs for both batches."

Words at **WORK**

The following workplace terms are used in this chapter and are defined in the Glossary at the back of this book. If you do not know a word, first try to get the meaning by looking at it in context. Then consider any prefix, suffix, or root. If the meaning is still not clear, look it up in the Glossary.

- Celsius
- dietitian
- Fahrenheit
- geriatric facility
- gross
- Medicaid
- purchase order
- reimburse
- supplier
- trade association
- warranty

Melanie sighed. She knew the mistake wasn't her fault. She didn't think that Sunset House should have to pay for it. On the other hand, was it worth getting into an argument about? After all, shipping couldn't be more than $20.

APPLYING **COMMUNICATION** SKILLS

Write your answers to the following questions.

1. What is the main communication problem between Melanie and Herman?

   _____
   _____
   _____

2. What might have caused it?

   _____
   _____
   _____

3. What are some possible solutions to the problem?

   _____
   _____
   _____
   _____
   _____

4. Select the one solution that you think best. Why would you suggest that Melanie try it?

   _____
   _____
   _____
   _____
   _____

Workplace Success

5. How might Melanie avoid having similar problems in the future?

_____

_____

_____

_____

6. Suppose Melanie were to write Herman about this problem. What points do you think she should make in her letter? Jot down your ideas.

_____

_____

_____

_____

_____

_____

Check your answers on page 132.

LESSON 1 Writing to Persuade

Persuasive writing convinces the reader to take action, or to support an idea. In a persuasive paragraph, the main idea is your opinion on the topic. It is usually stated in a topic sentence. The other sentences support this opinion with reasons, facts, and evidence. The purpose of a persuasive paragraph is to get your reader to agree with you. You might also want your reader to do something.

Before you write a persuasive paragraph, it's important to think about your audience. The facts and reasons you stress will depend on what is most important to the readers you are trying to convince. Try to predict what these readers' objections are likely to be. In your paragraph, include reasons that will overcome each of these objections.

The tone of a persuasive paragraph should be strong, but polite. People are not likely to do what you suggest if you insult or make fun of them. For example, telling readers that only a stupid fool would disagree with you is not likely to win them over.

EXAMPLE

Look at the example of a persuasive paragraph from someone who is applying for a job at Sunset House.

> I am sure that I would be an outstanding nursing assistant at Sunset House. If you hire me, you will be very satisfied with your choice. Although I have never worked in a **geriatric facility** before, many of the patients at Memorial Hospital are elderly. I am familiar with the special needs of elderly patients. I enjoy working with these patients, and found it very satisfying to be able to help them. At Memorial Hospital, I also assist in many medical procedures. I communicate often with staff members and patients' families. So, I have developed technical and communications skills that make me an outstanding nursing assistant.

1. What is the purpose of the letter?

   _____
   _____

2. What facts does the letter include?

   _____
   _____
   _____
   _____
   _____
   _____

3. What possible objection does the writer raise?

   _____

4. How does the writer overcome that objection?

   _____
   _____

Check your answers on page 132.

Workplace Success 55

EXERCISE 1 Get Your Point Across

Imagine that Mr. Hogarth recently visited Sunset House in order to decide whether or not his father would like to live there. You are following up on the visit with a letter to Mr. Hogarth. Your purpose is to convince him that Sunset House is the right place for his father.

Write *P* next to the facts from the list below that you think are reasons that would persuade Mr. Hogarth. Write *O* next to facts that he might see as objections. Put a *X* next to the facts that are neither persuasive nor objectionable.

_____ 1. Sunset House has nurses 24-hours a day, and a house physician is on call at all times.

_____ 2. Sunset House is the most expensive nursing facility in the county.

_____ 3. Most residents of Sunset House have a serious medical condition.

_____ 4. The staff at Sunset House is friendly.

_____ 5. All residents have private rooms.

_____ 6. Residents who choose to may furnish their rooms with their own possessions.

_____ 7. The staff **dietitian** plans all menus, and special meals are prepared for patients with special needs.

_____ 8. There is a lake on the property.

_____ 9. Sunset House is located ten miles from the nearest hospital.

_____ 10. All residents of Sunset House can participate in recreational therapy.

_____ 11. Physical therapy is available for residents who need it.

_____ 12. The lounge has a library, bridge tables, cards and games, and conversation areas.

_____ 13. The dining room is painted a bright blue and has travel posters on the wall.

_____ 14. Juice is served in the morning and hot drinks and snacks are available in the afternoon.

_____ 15. Coffee, tea, and cocoa are served in the lounge in the evening.

Check your answers on page 133.

EXERCISE 2 Put It All Together

Check your answers on page 133.

Use facts from the list in Exercise 1 to write a paragraph that will persuade Mr. Hogarth to admit his father to Sunset House. Use a separate sheet of paper for your paragraph.

LESSON 2 Writing to Complain

When things go wrong at work, you may find that writing a **complaint** will set them right. When you write a complaint, you are really asking somebody to do something to correct a situation. Therefore, complaints are a form of persuasive writing. The first thing you should do when writing to complain is think about what you want your reader to do. The objective of the paragraph should be to get the reader to correct the problem. You can follow these three steps to reach this objective:

1. State the problem.
2. Explain why it is a problem.
3. Tell your reader what you want done to solve the problem.

EXAMPLE

Let's look at a real-life example of a one-paragraph complaint. It comes from a letter to Mr. Demasi's nephew.

> We still have not received the forms we gave you to fill out when you first brought your uncle to Sunset House. As we explained at the time, these forms are necessary for **Medicaid** to reimburse us for the cost of your uncle's stay here. You may not be aware that we have a very tight budget and depend on payments from Medicaid to meet our expenses. Therefore, we must receive the forms as soon as possible. In case you lost the set we gave you, we are enclosing another set. We would appreciate it if you would fill them out and return them to us immediately.

1. What is the problem?

   _____

2. Why is it a problem?

   _____

   _____

Workplace Success 57

Check your answers on page 133.

3. What is the writer asking the reader to do to solve the problem?

_____

_____

EXERCISE 1 Identify the Problem

Think about the situation below. Then answer the questions that follow.

Ten weeks ago, Sunset House ordered a whirlpool bath from the Relaxercise Corporation. The equipment worked fine until about a week ago, when it became impossible to control the water pressure. Since the pressure is set differently for different residents, this control is very important. Because it is broken, Sunset House cannot use the whirlpool bath. The whirlpool bath came with **warranty.** The warranty guaranteed that the bath would be replaced or repaired within 90 days, unless the problem was caused by misuse. You know the bath had been used correctly.

1. What's the problem?

_____

_____

2. Why is it a problem?

_____

_____

3. What do you want the reader to do about the problem?

_____

_____

_____

_____

Check your answers on page 133.

58   Chapter 6   Kinds of Paragraphs: Persuasive

EXERCISE 2 Ask for a Solution

Check your answers on page 133.

Use the information from Exercise 1 to write a paragraph of complaint to the Relaxercise Corporation. Use a separate sheet of paper.

LESSON 3 Writing to Threaten Action

Complaints do not always lead to a solution. If you have made a complaint more than once, and the person you are complaining to does not correct the situation, you may have to threaten action. Appropriate threats are that you will withhold payment, take your business elsewhere, complain to a **trade association,** or take legal action.

A paragraph making such a threat is very much like a paragraph of complaint. However, you end the paragraph by telling the reader what you action you intend to take if the problem is not solved.

Example:

Look at the example of a paragraph that contains an appropriate threat. Think about how it differs from the complaint paragraph on page 59. Also, ask yourself what the problem is, and what action the writer threatens to take.

> We wrote to you three weeks ago requesting that you fill out some forms regarding your uncle, Ralph Demasi, who is a resident here. To date, we have not received the forms. As we explained previously, if we do not have these forms, we cannot collect payment from Medicaid. If we do not hear from you by the end of the month, we will no longer be able to let your uncle stay at Sunset House.

In this case, the problem is still that Mr. Demasi's nephew did not fill out the forms. The threat is that Mr. Demasi will not be allowed to remain at Sunset House. Did you notice that the tone is stronger than the previous paragraph?

EXERCISE 1 Choose Your Weapon

Think about the situation below. Then answer the questions that follow

> Arlene Adams is a representative from the Relaxercise Corporation. She called after receiving your letter (Exercise 2 of Lesson 2, page 59) about the defective whirlpool bath. She promised to come and inspect it. However, Ms. Adams keeps delaying her visit. Another month has passed, and the whirlpool bath is still broken.

1. What is the problem?
   _____
   _____

2. Why is it a problem?
   _____
   _____

3. What do you want the reader to do about the problem?
   _____
   _____
   _____
   _____

4. What threat do you think would be most appropriate?
   _____
   _____

Check your answers on page 133.

EXERCISE 2 Demand Action

Check your answers on page 133.

Use the information from Exercise 1 to write a paragraph of complaint to the Relaxercise Corporation. Use a separate sheet of paper.

60   Chapter 6   Kinds of Paragraphs: Persuasive

FOR YOUR Portfolio

PERSUADE PEOPLE TO ACT

Your assignment is to write two paragraphs to Mr. Broadman about the thermometers (see page 52).

1. Assume that you were unable to resolve the problem about the shipping costs. In the first paragraph, write to Mr. Broadman to complain.

_____
_____
_____
_____
_____
_____
_____
_____
_____

2. Assume that Mr. Broadman did not do anything about your complaint. Write a paragraph in which you threaten to take action unless he resolves the problem.

_____
_____
_____
_____
_____
_____
_____
_____
_____

Workplace Success

CHAPTER 7

On the Job: Designer Clothing Company

Kinds of Correspondence: Memos, E-Mail, Faxes, and Messages

SOLVING COMMUNICATION PROBLEMS

While Jason tried to catch up on his filing, he kept an ear open for the explosion that he knew was coming. Soon enough, he heard what he was waiting for.

"What? What in the world…! She must me out of her mind!" roared Steve Hart, as he stormed around his tiny office, waving his arms.

"Jason!" shouted Steve from his office, "Jason, get Yoli on the phone!"

When Jason had put the **memo** on Steve's desk earlier that morning, he knew what the day would bring. Steve had wanted facts and figures that would convince the bank to lend them money for the new **sergers.** He needed to know how the sergers that Yoli recommended would increase **productivity.** He also needed to know how quickly productivity gains would pay for the **investment.**

Steve was a numbers man. This kind of information was as natural to him as breathing. Yoli was a designer. Instead of facts and figures, Yoli's memo stressed the different weight fabrics the new sergers could handle and the ease of operating them. She wrote about how the new machines might even lead her to create more exciting dresses. Steve wasn't pleased with the focus of Yoli's memo, and that is why he was screaming.

Words at WORK

The following workplace terms are used in this chapter and are defined in the Glossary at the back of this book. If you do not know a word, first try to get the meaning by looking at it in context. Then consider any prefix, suffix, or root. If the meaning is still not clear, look it up in the Glossary.

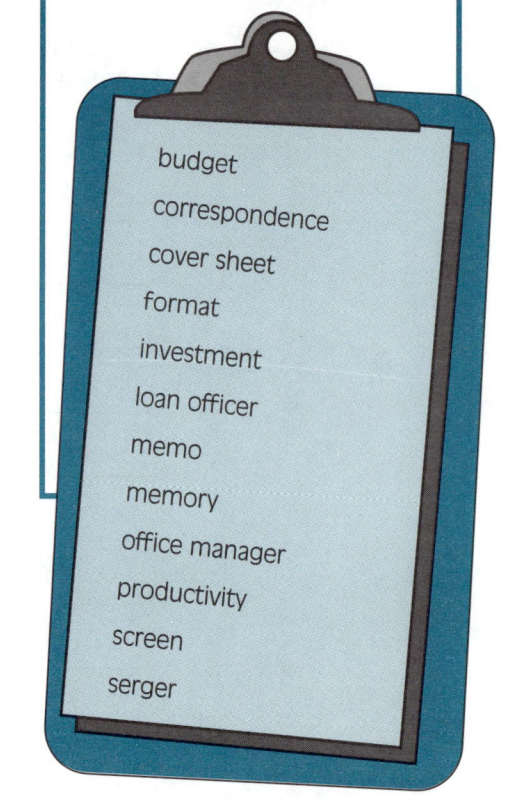

budget
correspondence
cover sheet
format
investment
loan officer
memo
memory
office manager
productivity
screen
serger

APPLYING COMMUNICATION SKILLS

Write your answers to the following questions.

1. What is the main communication problem between Yoli and Steve?
   _____
   _____

2. What might have caused it?
   _____
   _____
   _____
   _____

3. What are some possible solutions to the problem?
   _____
   _____
   _____
   _____
   _____
   _____
   _____

4. Select the one solution you think is best. Why would you suggest that Steve try it?
   _____
   _____
   _____
   _____
   _____
   _____
   _____

Workplace Success

5. Some companies put together teams of employees from different departments and different levels. These teams get together to find solutions to problems and ways to make the company run better. What do you think some advantages might be of using such teams? How could they have helped to avoid a problem like the one Steve and Yoli are having?

_____

_____

_____

Check your answers on page 133.

_____

_____

_____

LESSON 1 Memos

At work, you use memos to communicate with people within and outside your company. The main difference between a memo and other forms of written communication is its **format.** The memo has a standard format for presenting key information including the following headings:

- **TO:** The person to whom the message is addressed
- **FROM:** The person from whom the message is coming
- **DATE:** The date the message is written
- **SUBJECT:** The subject of the message or **RE:** ("Regarding")

Some people may type memos on preprinted forms that already contain the headings. Others may type on plain paper and add the headings themselves. In either case, the headings are followed by the message. The message may be as short as a sentence, or as long as a few pages. A memo message is generally written in a businesslike tone. However, it may be less formal than a business letter.

Example:

Let's look at a real-life example of a memo. When you read it, think about why the memo form is useful for the person who will receive the memo.

Also notice that the memo has the Ms. Sensation, Inc. name and logo printed on it, along with the words *Interoffice Memo*. Since the memo is meant for communications within the company, the address and phone number are omitted.

Ms. Sensation, Inc.

INTEROFFICE MEMO

To: Steve Hart
From: Yoli Kroll
Date: August 20, 199—
Subject: Simplex Model 21346 Sergers

The Simplex Model 21346 Serger is the answer to my prayers! It is fast and quiet. It works on may kinds of fabrics. Yes, Steve, it costs a lot more than we **budgeted,** but still, we should buy at least six now. We need them to handle the heavyweight wool fabrics in the winter line as well as the terrycloth and spandex that I am planning for next summer.

These sergers are much easier to operate than any others I have seen. This means that our sewing machine operators will be able to take on fancier stitches than than they can now. With so much more variety, I can't even begin to imagine the wonderful clothes I will design!

Did you notice how easy it is for the reader to see who the memo is from and what it is about? Later on, if the reader wants to review the memo, it will be easy to know when it was written.

EXERCISE 1 Write a Memo

Check your answers on page 133.

Steve has asked Jason to reserve the conference room in order to hold a meeting with Yoli and the **loan officer** from the bank. In order to reserve the conference room, Jason must write a memo to the **office manager,** Libby Cadley. He wants to hold his meeting on August 23 at 10 AM. Jason is writing the memo on August 20. Use a separate sheet of paper to write the memo for Jason.

LESSON 2 E-Mail and Fax Communications

In recent years, new technology has made it possible to send messages in a flash. Two fairly new forms of communication are e-mail and faxes. With e-mail you can send a written message from your computer to another computer. The message or file you send can be used with word processors and other computer tools. With a fax, you can send a

Workplace Success   65

print out of a written message through your telephone lines. The person receiving a fax would have to retype it, if it had to be added to another document.

Faxes and e-mail messages are memos, even though they are sent in a different way. Like memos, they use standard formats for listing key information above the message. When you send a fax, you will need to include the information shown in the following list. The page that contains this information is called the **cover sheet.**

- The date of the message
- The person to whom you are sending the message
- That person's fax number
- The person from whom the message is coming
- That person's fax and phone numbers
- The number of pages

Sometimes you will only be sending a short message that will fit on the fax cover sheet itself. On other occasions, you may send a memo, letter, or report along with the cover sheet. Therefore, it is important to include the number of pages. Otherwise, the person on the other end will not know when the last page has been received. Be sure to include the cover sheet when you count the pages.

With e-mail, the computer will add some of the key information automatically. Therefore, the communication will contain items that you did not actually type. The following list includes all the key items that make up the e-mail heading. Note which ones you need to provide, and which ones the computer provides automatically.

- *The person who sent the message.* This is provided by the computer.
- *The date of the message.* This is provided by the computer.
- *The time of the message.* This is provided by the computer.
- *The person, or people, to whom the message is being sent.* A company's e-mail system probably lists the electronic addresses of its employees. Select their names from this list in the computer's **memory,** rather than typing them onto the e-mail **screen.**

To send e-mail outside your company, call the addressee and get the complete e-mail address. Your system may be able to store this address for future use.

- *The names of people who should receive copies.* Some systems allow you to send copies to other people. As with the name of the person to whom the message is going, you select these from the address list.
- *Subject of the message.* You write this yourself. For some e-mail systems, there is a limit to how long the subject line can be.
- *The message.* You write this yourself.

You can write the entire message on the e-mail screen, or you can have the computer attach other documents that are in the computer's memory.

Figure 7-1
There are many e-mail systems. What you see on the screen when you send a message will depend on the system you use. The screen to the right is typical.

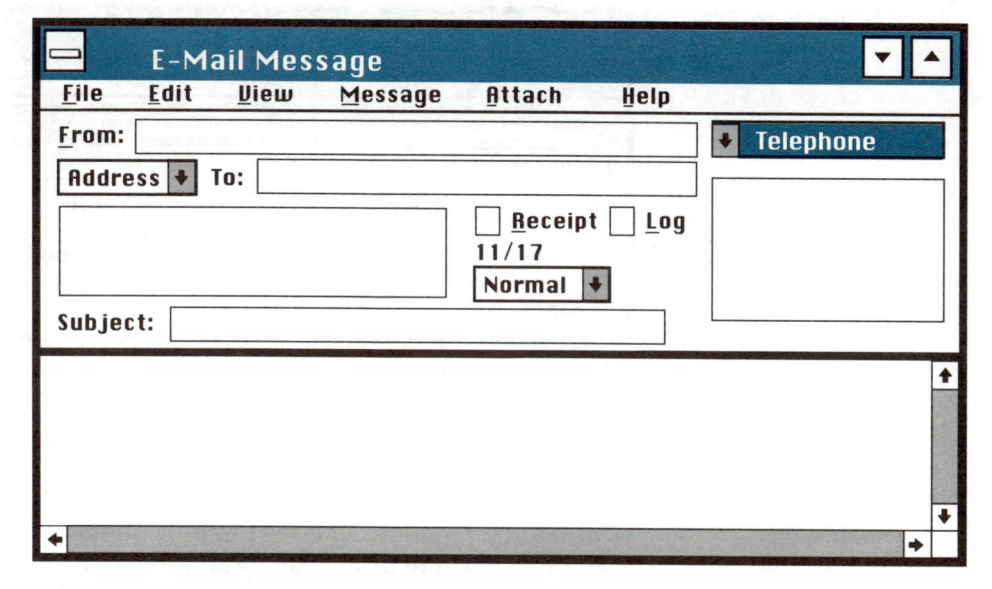

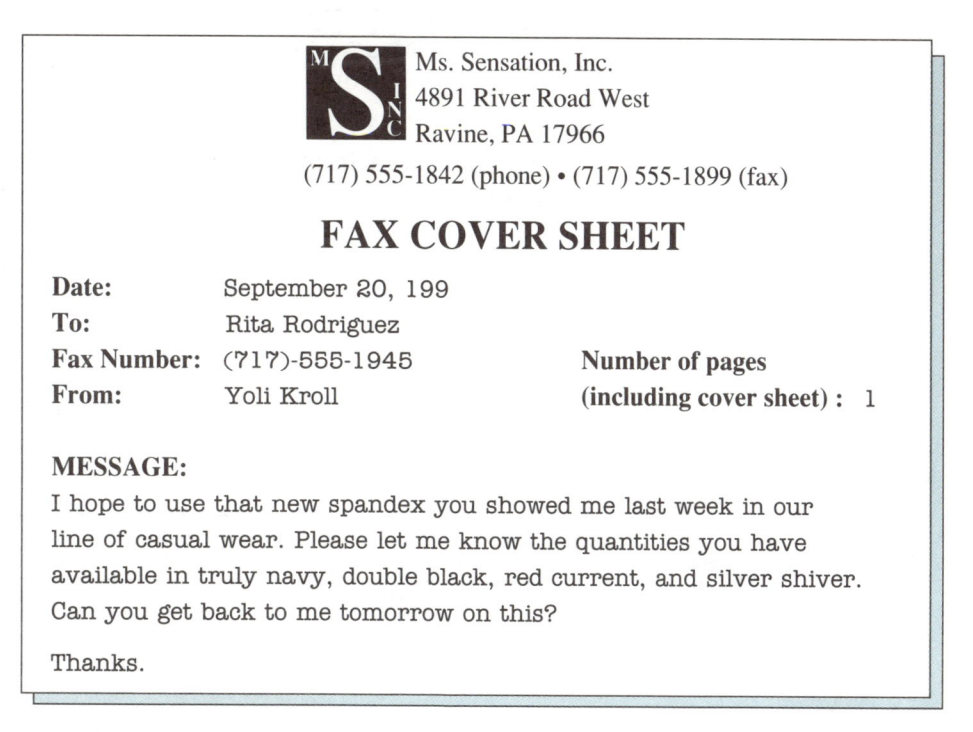

[E-Mail Message window showing fields: From, To, Address, Subject, Receipt, Log, 11/17, Normal, Telephone, with menu items File, Edit, View, Message, Attach, Help]

With both e-mail and fax communications, you should keep the message as short as possible. If you plan to attach a lengthy document, you should call the person beforehand to make sure he or she wants you to send it. Also remember that both e-mail and fax communications are more public than **correspondence** that travels inside an envelope. Fax messages will be seen by anyone who happens to be at the machine when they come in. E-mail can be viewed by anybody on that particular computer system. Therefore, be sure to keep these messages businesslike. Do not to say anything in them that cannot be said publicly.

EXAMPLE

Let's look at a real-life example of the same message sent by fax and e-mail. Yoli faxed the message to her sales representative at a fabric manufacturer. As a reminder, she also e-mailed the message to the sales rep's address at Ms. Sensation. Yoli wanted to make sure that the fabric she needed was available in large quantities.

Figure 7-2
Fax Message

> Ms. Sensation, Inc.
> 4891 River Road West
> Ravine, PA 17966
>
> (717) 555-1842 (phone) • (717) 555-1899 (fax)
>
> ### FAX COVER SHEET
>
> Date: September 20, 199
> To: Rita Rodriguez
> Fax Number: (717)-555-1945   **Number of pages**
> From: Yoli Kroll   **(including cover sheet) :** 1
>
> **MESSAGE:**
> I hope to use that new spandex you showed me last week in our line of casual wear. Please let me know the quantities you have available in truly navy, double black, red current, and silver shiver. Can you get back to me tomorrow on this?
>
> Thanks.

Workplace Success   67

Figure 7-3
E-mail Message

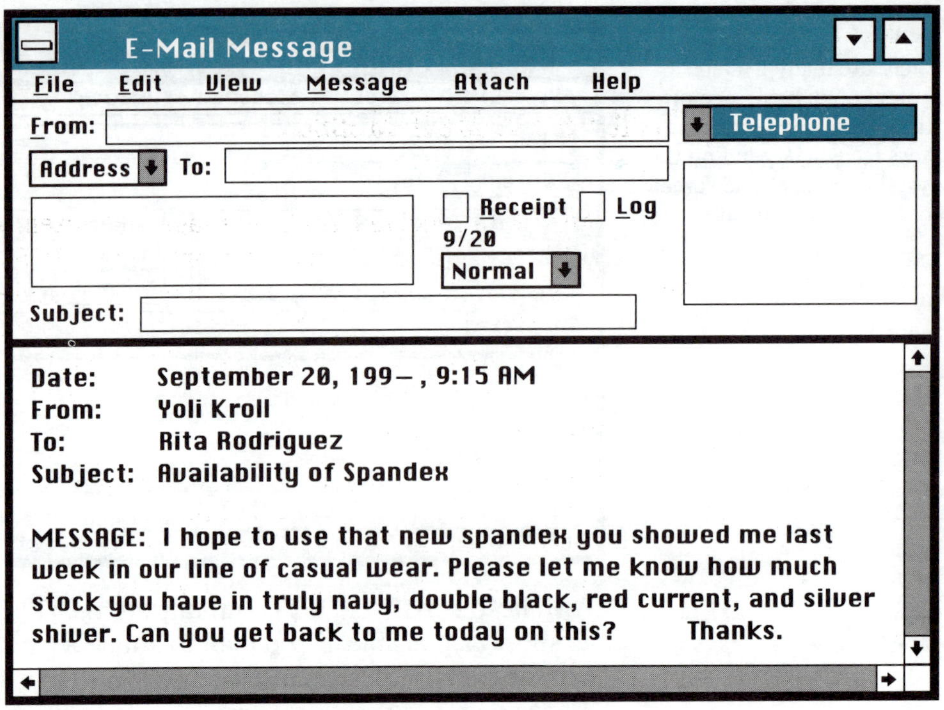

```
┌─────────────────────────────────────────────────────────────┐
│ ▭          E-Mail Message                            ▼  ▲  │
│ File   Edit   View   Message   Attach   Help                │
│ From: [_____]          ▼ Telephone       │
│ [Address ▼] To: [_____]   ┌──────────┐       │
│ ┌──────────────┐      ☐ Receipt ☐ Log   │          │       │
│ │              │  9/20                   │          │       │
│ │              │  [Normal ▼]             │          │       │
│ └──────────────┘                          └──────────┘       │
│ Subject: [_____]                         │
├─────────────────────────────────────────────────────────────┤
│ Date:      September 20, 199— , 9:15 AM                     │
│ From:      Yoli Kroll                                       │
│ To:        Rita Rodriguez                                   │
│ Subject:   Availability of Spandex                          │
│                                                             │
│ MESSAGE: I hope to use that new spandex you showed me last  │
│ week in our line of casual wear. Please let me know how much│
│ stock you have in truly navy, double black, red current, and│
│ silver shiver. Can you get back to me today on this? Thanks.│
└─────────────────────────────────────────────────────────────┘
```

1. Write *F* if the item appears only in the fax message, *E* if it appears only in the e-mail message, and *B* if it appears in both.

    _____ a. Name of sender

    _____ b. Name of recipient

    _____ c. Fax number

    _____ d. Date

    _____ e. Subject line

    _____ f. Number of pages

2. Which item or items in the e-mail message were typed in by the sender?

    _____

    _____

3. What information is provided on a fax form that is not provided in a regular memo heading?

    _____

    _____

Check your answers on page 134.

68   Chapter 7   Kinds of Correspondence: Memos, E-Mail, Faxes, and Messages

EXERCISE 1 Write an E-Mail Message

After Rita received Yoli's message on September 20, she checked the inventory for the items Yoli wanted. By 11:15, she had found out that there were 60 bolts (rolls) of truly navy spandex, 45 bolts of red currant, 29 bolts of double-black, and five bolts of silver shiver in stock. She also found out that additional bolts could be manufactured within three weeks of the date it is ordered. She decided to e-mail this information to Yoli right away.

On a separate sheet of paper, make up a form like that in Figure 7-3. It will show what Rita sees on her computer screen when she sends an e-mail message. Fill in the information for Rita. Don't fill in the information that the computer will provide.

Check your answers on page 134.

EXERCISE 2 Visualize an E-Mail Message

When Yoli receives the e-mail message from Rita, what will it look like? In the space below, write what Yoli will see on the screen of her computer.

Check your answers on page 134.

Workplace Success   69

EXERCISE 3 Send a Fax

Check your answers on page 134.

When Yoli got Rita's e-mail message, she was glad to see that Rita's company had all the red, navy, and black spandex she would need. She would, however, need more silver. She decided to send Rita a fax immediately. She wanted Rita to reserve ten bolts each of red currant, truly navy, and double-black spandex. She also wanted Rita to reserve all five bolts of silver shiver and to order her an additional five bolts. Rita's fax number is (717) 555-1945. Yoli's fax number is (717) 555-1842. Her phone number is (717) 555-1899. Write Yoli's fax on a separate sheet of paper. Include all the boldface headings in Figure 7-2 on page 67.

LESSON 3 Telephone Messages

Telephone messages are very short memos with a single purpose—to tell people about phone calls they have received. Most businesses use standard forms for taking telephone messages. These forms include spaces for the following information:

- Who the message is for
- The date and time the call was received
- Who the message is from
- That person's company or department
- The person's telephone number, including the area code and extension
- What the message is
- Who took the message

Even if your company does not use a preprinted form, you should include all of the information in the list above when you take a telephone message. (Do not include the complete phone number of people within the company, if you only have to dial the extension.)

Some telephone message forms include a list of items that can be marked with a check or an *X*. This form is handy because you do not have to write common messages such as "Wants you to call," or "Will call you again." The form also allows the person who receives the message to scan it quickly.

When you take telephone messages, listen carefully. Ask callers to repeat anything you do not understand. Also feel free to ask them to spell their names. Listen especially carefully to telephone numbers, and repeat them back to the caller. You may want to take notes on a scrap of paper as you listen, then use your notes when you write up the message.

EXAMPLE   Let's look at two real-life examples of telephone messages for Steve Hart. Jason took the one on the left. Sally Drumm, the receptionist, took the one on the right.

```
         TELEPHONE MESSAGE
  TO: Steve
  DATE: 8/22        TIME: 10:15 AM
  M Yoli
  OF _____
  TEL. NO. x899
           (AREA CODE)

  Telephoned         ✓   Wishes to see you
  Please return call ✓   Wishes appointment
  Returned your call     Urgent
  Will call again        Messages (below)  ✓

  She wants to know if you've
  heard from the bank about
  the meeting.

                              Jason
```

```
         TELEPHONE MESSAGE
  TO: Steve Hart
  DATE: 8/22        TIME: 1:15 PM
  M r. Roberto Longo
  OF Brookside National Bank
  TEL. NO. (717) 555-3825
           (AREA CODE)

  Telephoned         ✓   Wishes to see you
  Please return call     Wishes appointment
  Returned your call     Urgent
  Will call again    ✓   Messages (below)  ✓

  He will be out of the
  office most of the
  afternoon.

                          Sally Drumm
```

1. Who telephoned first, Yoli or Mr. Longo?

   _____

2. What did Yoli want Steve to do?

   _____
   _____

3. Why did she want to speak to Steve?

   _____
   _____

4. Why do you think Mr. Longo did not ask Steve to call him back?

   _____
   _____
   _____

Workplace Success

5. Why do you think Jason used only first names in his memo, and left off the name of Yoli's department?

_____

_____

Check your answers on page 134.

6. Why do you think Jason left off Yoli's complete phone number?

_____

_____

EXERCISE 1 Write a Telephone Message

When Mr. Longo called Steve back, he told Steve that he could come to the meeting on August 23 at 10 AM. Unfortunately, Yoli was not at her desk when Steve called at 4:30 PM. to let her know about the meeting. Sally Drumm, the receptionist, picked up the call. Steve gave Sally the information to pass on to Yoli. Write the telephone message for Sally on the form below.

```
              TELEPHONE MESSAGE

TO: _____
DATE: _____  TIME: _____
   M _____
   OF _____
   TEL. NO. _____
               (AREA CODE)

| Telephoned         |   | Wishes to see you   |   |
| Please return call |   | Wishes appointment  |   |
| Returned your call |   | Urgent              |   |
| Will call again    |   | Messages (below)    |   |

............................................
............................................
............................................
............................................
                                    _____
```

Check your answers on page 134.

72   Chapter 7   Kinds of Correspondence: Memos, E-Mail, Faxes, and Messages

FOR YOUR Portfolio

WRITE A MEMO OUTLINING A PLAN

Write a memo to Steve Hart, suggesting that Ms. Sensation, Inc. start using teams of employees like the ones described in question 5 on page 64. At this point, you want Steve to know why you think this is a good idea. Specific plans for setting up the teams can come later. Write your memo on the memo form below.

Ms. Sensation, Inc.

INTEROFFICE MEMO

To:
From:
Date:
Subject:

CHAPTER 8

On the Job: Designer Clothing Company

Kinds of Correspondence: Letters

SOLVING COMMUNICATION PROBLEMS

Jason spoke to Yoli himself before he put Steve on the phone.

"Yoli," he said, "Steve is having a fit over your memo! Didn't you know what he would want? Can't you just give him some numbers to make him feel better?"

"Oh, Jason, Jason, Jason," Yoli said. Jason could tell she was trying hard not to show her anger. "I just can't do it. He's always asking for these things. But I don't understand them. It's not my language. It's not my concern. I just want to design wonderful dresses that our customers will love. It's my dresses that make Ms. Sensation so popular with teenage girls."

Jason offered to help. "We can stay late tonight," he told Yoli. "I'm sure we can come up with something that Steve will like. It's not really that hard."

"It's no use, Jason," Yoli replied, "Tonight is Randy's Cub Scout meeting, and I have to get home by 6 o'clock." Yoli was silent for a moment. "But I do appreciate all your help," she added.

Jason could hear the slight edge in Yoli's voice. "You don't sound like you appreciate it," he told her.

"It's just that sometimes I don't understand you. You're as sweet as can be with me—always ready to help. But you let Steve say anything he pleases behind my back. Did you ever once come to my defense?"

"But Yoli," Jason sighed, "Steve's my boss."

"*I'm* your friend," Yoli asserted, "Doesn't that stand for anything?"

At moments like this, Jason wished he could just up and quit his job. Unfortunately, he couldn't. He needed his salary, and his **medical insurance**.

Words at WORK

The following workplace terms are used in this chapter and are defined in the Glossary at the back of this book. If you do not know a word, first try to get the meaning by looking at it in context. Then consider any prefix, suffix, or root. If the meaning is still not clear, look it up in the Glossary.

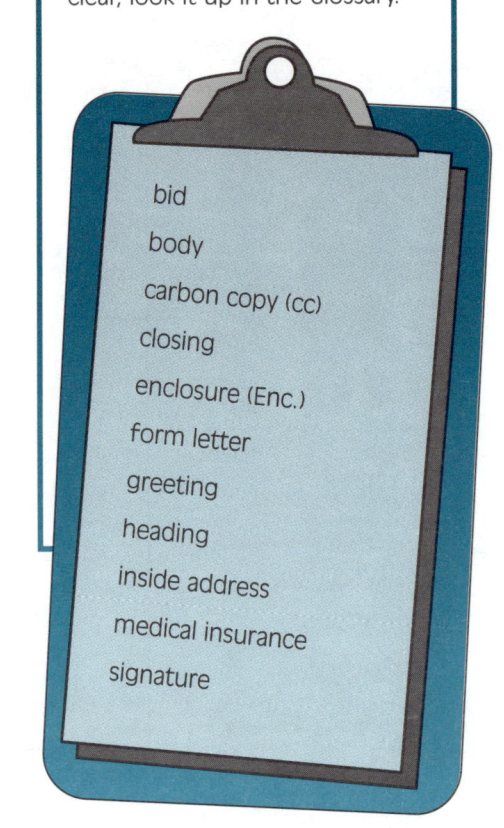

- bid
- body
- carbon copy (cc)
- closing
- enclosure (Enc.)
- form letter
- greeting
- heading
- inside address
- medical insurance
- signature

APPLYING COMMUNICATION SKILLS

Write your answers to the following questions.

1. What is the main communication problem between Yoli and Jason?

   _____
   _____
   _____

2. What might have caused it?

   _____
   _____
   _____
   _____

3. What are some possible solutions to the problem?

   _____
   _____
   _____
   _____
   _____

4. Select the one solution you think is best. Why would you suggest that Jason try it?

   _____
   _____
   _____
   _____
   _____

Workplace Success

5. Jason seems to be caught in a personality clash between Yoli and Steve. What advice would you give Jason if he asked you what to do? Write your ideas on the following lines.

_____
_____
_____
_____
_____
_____
_____

Check your answers on page 134.

LESSON 1 Heading, Inside Address, and Greeting

Business letters follow a certain standard form. The core of the letter, or **body,** is made up of one or more paragraphs. These paragraphs contain the message you want to communicate. Your letter also needs the following features above the body:

1. *Heading.* The **heading** of a business letter contains the name and address of the company sending the letter and the date the letter is written. For letters on stationery with the company's name and address printed on it, the heading includes only the date.

2. *Inside address.* The **inside address** gives the name and address of the person that the letter is going to. This person is the recipient.

3. *Greeting.* The **greeting** is made up of the word "Dear," a title such as "Mr.," "Miss," "Mrs.," "Ms.," or "Dr.," and the last name of the recipient. When you do not know the name of the recipient, you can address the letter to the title of the person you want to reach or the name of the department or company. For example, you might write "Dear Marketing Director" or "Dear Dwight's Department Stores." You can also use the greeting, "To Whom It May Concern."

Note that business letters are not always written at work. For example, you might write a letter from home to apply for a job or ask for information from a company. You should use the business-letter format for such letters. (Of course, you would not include a company name in the heading. Instead you would include your name and home address.)

76   Chapter 8   Kinds of Correspondence: Letters

EXAMPLE

Let's look at a real-life example of the opening sections of a business letter.

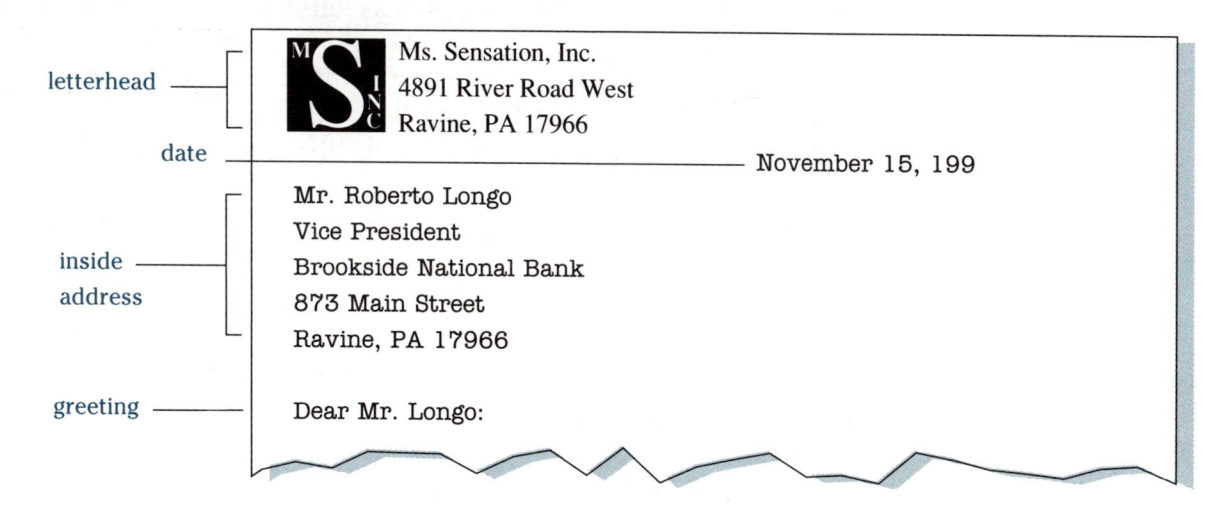

letterhead — Ms. Sensation, Inc.
4891 River Road West
Ravine, PA 17966

date — November 15, 199

inside address —
Mr. Roberto Longo
Vice President
Brookside National Bank
873 Main Street
Ravine, PA 17966

greeting — Dear Mr. Longo:

1. Which standard feature appears on the right side of the paper?

   _____
   _____

2. In addition to the address, what information is in the inside address?

   _____
   _____

Check your answers on page 134.

3. Why isn't the company name and address included in this heading?

   _____
   _____

EXERCISE 1 Begin a Letter

Check your answers on page 134.

Suppose you wanted to write a letter to Ms. Sensation to ask for information about job openings. The human resources department will probably have the information you want. You do not know the name of the person to whom the letter should be addressed. On a separate sheet of paper, write the heading, inside address, and greeting for your letter. Use your own address and today's date in the heading.

Workplace Success   77

LESSON 2 The Closing of the Letter

After you write the body of a business letter, you end it with a closing. The **closing** contains a polite word or phrase, such as "Sincerely," or "Cordially yours," and your signature. The **signature** is made up of your typewritten name, with your handwritten name above it. If you are writing your letter from work, your title should be typed below your name.

In some letters, you will need to add other features below the closing. If you are sending copies of the letter to other people, you add a **cc** (**carbon copy,** or duplicate) line. This is done by typing "cc:" followed by the name or names of the people being copied. If you are sending anything along with the letter, you indicate that there is an enclosure. You do so by typing either "**Enclosure**" or the abbreviation "**Enc.**" You might also add a listing of the item or items that are enclosed.

EXAMPLE

Let's look at a real-life example of the bottom section of a business letter.

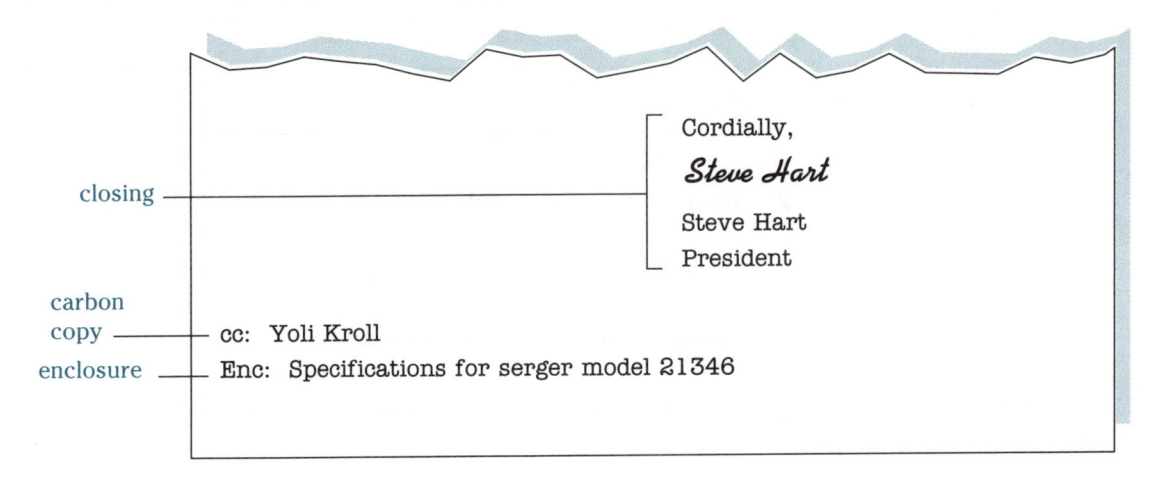

closing:
Cordially,
Steve Hart
Steve Hart
President

carbon copy: cc: Yoli Kroll

enclosure: Enc: Specifications for serger model 21346

1. What is Steve Hart's title? Where can you find this information?

   _____

2. Who is going to receive a copy of this letter? How do you know?

   _____

   _____

Check your answers on page 135.

3. What will be sent with the letter? How do you know?

   _____

   _____

   _____

78 Chapter 8 Kinds of Correspondence: Letters

EXERCISE 1 Close a Letter

Write the closing to your letter to the human resources department below. You do not intend to send anybody copies of your letter. You will enclose your resume and photocopies of some sketches of dress designs you made.

_____
_____
_____
_____
_____
_____

Check your answers on page 135.

Figure 8–1
A complete business letter in standard form.

Ms. Sensation, Inc.
4891 River Road West
Ravine, PA 17966

November 15, 199

Mr. Roberto Longo
Vice President
Brookside National Bank
873 Main Street
Ravine, PA 17966

Dear Mr. Longo:

You asked why we chose serger model 21346. Our main reason is that it works well with a large variety of fabrics. Since we plan to use spandex and terrycloth in our next line, we need this flexibility.

In addition, model 21346 is the most advanced machine on the market. (See enclosed specifications.) It is 9 percent faster than the next fastest machine. It is also 12 percent quieter. This serger is easier to handle than others we tested. It has advanced safty devices.

The use of these machines will make our factory more efficient and safer.

Cordially,

Steve Hart

Steve Hart
President

cc: Yoli Kroll
Enc: Specifications for serger model 21346

Workplace Success

LESSON 3 Envelopes and Labels

The envelopes you use for business letters should follow a certain format. Your name and return address should appear in the upper left-hand corner. If the envelope has the name and address of your company printed on it, you will not need to type a return address. You may, however, want to add your name above the printed address. The recipient's address includes the recipient's name, his or her title, company name, and mailing address. It should be printed in the center of the envelope. Be sure both addresses contain ZIP codes, and use the standard two-letter abbreviations for the names of states. These abbreviations are found in telephone directories. You can also get them from your post office.

You can send most letters in standard-size business envelopes (called "Number 10" envelopes). Sometimes, however, your letter will be accompanied by materials that are too big to fit in such an envelope. In these cases, you can use a larger-sized envelope. Attach a label with the address typed on it. You can follow the same format for the label that you use on the envelope.

EXAMPLE

Let's look at a real-life example of an envelope for a business letter.

```
MS INC   Steve Hart
         Ms. Sensation, Inc.
         4891 River Road West
         Ravine, PA 17966

                        Mr. Roberto Longo
                        Vice President
                        Brookside National Bank
                        873 Main Street
                        Ravine, PA 17966
```

1. What part of the business letter contains exactly the same information as the recipient's address on the envelope?

   _____

   _____

2. How would the envelope be different if Ms. Sensation did not have printed envelopes?

   _____

   _____

Check your answers on page 135.

EXERCISE 1 Address an Envelope

Using the following box as an envelope, address an envelope for your letter to the human resources department at Ms. Sensation.

Check your answers on page 135.

LESSON 4 Form Letters

Sometimes at work you will need to write the same letter to many different people. When this is the case, you can use a form letter. In a **form letter,** the message of the letter remains the same. This is the standardized part of the form letter. If you are sending out all copies of the form letter on the same day, the date can be part of the form as well. If not, the date should be changed each time you send out the letter. The inside address and greeting will change for each person. You might also individualize a small piece of information within the body of the letter. This individualized information will also change for each person.

With computers, it is easy to send out form letters. If you are not using a computer, you might retype the letter for each person. Or you might type the standardized part of the letter, leaving enough space to add the individualized information, and photocopy it. Then you can type in the individualized information on each photocopy. If you photocopy the letter and then type on it, the person who receives it will know it is a form letter. Therefore, you should only do this when recipients will not be offended by getting a form letter.

On the following page are real-life examples of a form letter at two stages: Example 1 is the form letter before it has been individualized. Example 2 is the letter after it has been individualized. Look for information in Example 2 that is not in Example 1.

Workplace Success   81

Example 1

Ms. Sensation, Inc.
4891 River Road West
Ravine, PA 17966

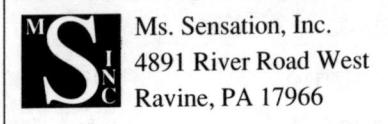

January 4, 199—

Dear   :

Ms. Sensation, Inc. has purchased six new Simplex model 21346 sergers. We are now seeking a supplier for parts that will keep our machines running well. We would be pleased to consider
If you would like to be considered, please send your bid to my attention by January 28, 199—.

Sincerely,

Jason Kramer
Administrative Assistant

Example 2

Ms. Sensation, Inc.
4891 River Road West
Ravine, PA 17966

January 4, 199—

Ms. Martha Magneson
Marketing Manager
KD Corporation
750 Ring Road North
Ravine, PA 17966

Dear Ms. Magneson:

Ms. Sensation, Inc. has purchased six new Simplex model 21346 sergers. We are now seeking a supplier for parts that will keep our machines running well. We would be pleased to consider KD Corporation. If you would like to be considered, please send your bid to my attention by January 28, 199—.

Sincerely,

Jason Kramer

Jason Kramer
Administrative Assistant

Did you notice that Example 2 included the inside address and greeting with the name and address of the particular company? Did you notice that the name of the company was added in the body itself?

EXERCISE 1 Complete a Form Letter

Jason will also ask Tucker Supplies, Inc. at 53 Market Street in Ravine, PA 17966, for a bid. He plans to write Leroy Benning, who is a vice president. Complete the form letter below for Jason.

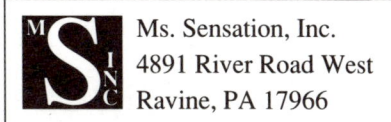

Ms. Sensation, Inc.
4891 River Road West
Ravine, PA 17966   January 4, 199—

Dear   :

Ms. Sensation, Inc. has purchased six new Simplex model 21346

sergers. We are now seeking a supplier for parts that will keep

our machines running well. We would be pleased to consider

                        . If you would like to be considered,

please send your bid to my attention by January 28, 199—.

Sincerely,

Jason Kramer

Jason Kramer
Administrative Assistant

Check your answers on page 135.

Workplace Success   83

FOR YOUR Portfolio

WRITE A LETTER

Write a letter to Jason Kramer at work. In the letter, give him your advice about how he can avoid being caught in the middle of Yoli and Steve. Use your own name and address and today's date in the heading. Use Jason's address and title of Administrative Assistant at Ms. Sensation, Inc. You will find the address in many of the examples in this chapter.

_____
_____
_____
_____
_____
_____
_____
_____
_____
_____
_____
_____
_____
_____
_____
_____
_____
_____
_____
_____

CHAPTER 9

On the Job: Designer Clothing Company

Forms

SOLVING COMMUNICATION PROBLEMS

Jason picked up the phone on the very first ring. "Mr. Hart's office," he announced.

"Is Mr. Hart in?" asked the voice at the other end.

"I'm afraid not," Jason said, "He's out to lunch. This is Jason Kramer, his assistant. May I help you?"

"Yes," the voice told Jason, "I guess maybe you can. This is Calvin Plant, from International Fashions. I want you to give Mr. Hart a message. I know he'll want to hear about it as soon as he gets in. Tell him everything went well at the **board meeting.** I think the deal will go through without a hitch."

"Certainly, Mr. Plant," Jason told him, "I'll be sure to give him the message as soon as he gets in."

"Thank you, Jason," Mr. Plant said before hanging up.

After Jason wrote up the message, he didn't go back to the typing he had been doing. Instead, he thought over Mr. Plant's words, "the deal will go through." What deal? Everything that Steve did passed through Jason's hands. How could there be a deal he didn't know about? What kind of deal could Ms. Sensation be making with a major company like International Fashions?

Jason began to put it together. Lately, not quite *everything* had been going through his hands. More and more often, Steve was telling Jason not to bother with certain file folders—that he would be taking care of this or that himself.

In a flash, Jason knew the answer. The only deal possible between International Fashions and a tiny company like Ms. Sensation was an **acquisition.** Ms. Sensation was about to be bought out, and Steve had not said a word about it to Jason!

Words at WORK

The following workplace terms are used in this chapter and are defined in the Glossary at the back of this book. If you do not know a word, first try to get the meaning by looking at it in context. Then consider any prefix, suffix, or root. If the meaning is still not clear, look it up in the Glossary.

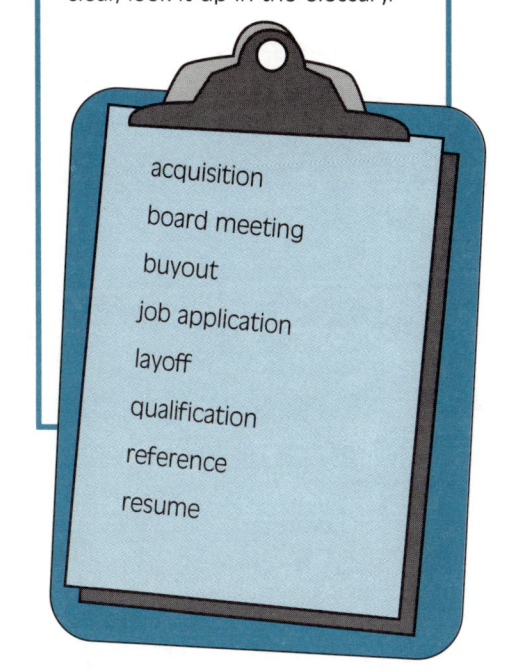

- acquisition
- board meeting
- buyout
- job application
- layoff
- qualification
- reference
- resume

85

Jason also knew what usually happens after **buyouts: layoffs.** "Well," Jason said to himself, "I'm not going to wait around to be fired." He grabbed a yellow pad and picked up his pen. "Let's see. What **qualifications** do I have that will help me land a good job?" he asked himself.

APPLYING COMMUNICATION SKILLS

Write your answers to the following questions.

1. What is the main communication problem between Jason and Steve?

   _____
   _____
   _____

2. What might have caused it?

   _____
   _____
   _____

3. What are some possible solutions to the problem?

   _____
   _____
   _____
   _____
   _____

4. Select the one solution you think is best. Why would you suggest that Jason try it?

   _____
   _____
   _____
   _____
   _____

5. Suppose you had to look for a new job. What experience and skills do you have that might help you get the job you want? Write down your ideas on the lines that follow.

_____

_____

_____

_____

_____

_____

Check your answers on page 135.

LESSON 1 Resumes

A **resume** is an essential job-hunting tool. It summarizes a person's job history. Employers find this information most helpful in deciding if an applicant has the right qualifications for a job.

There are many different styles for resumes, but most of them include the following:

1. *Heading.* The heading includes your name, address, and phone number. If you have a fax machine, it should include your fax number, too.

2. *Objective or Goal Statement.* The heading is followed by a brief goal statement that tells the type of job you are looking for.

3. *Experience.* In this section of the resume, you list the companies you have worked for. Start with your present, or most recent, employer. Give the dates of employment and a brief description of each job. In each job description, list your most important job responsibilities first.

4. *Education.* In this section, list the high school and college or technical school you have attended. Start with the most recent one. Also list any adult education courses you have taken.

5. *Skills.* Some people also include a section on the special skills that they will bring to a job. These might include knowledge of a foreign language, technical skills, computer skills, typing, and so forth.

6. *References.* Some people also include **references** on their resumes. They list two or three people who know them and have worked with them. The reference section should include the names, titles, addresses, and phone numbers for these people. Some people choose not to put their references on the resume. Instead, they state at the bottom of the resume that "References will be furnished upon request."

EXAMPLE

Let's look at a real-life example of a resume.

After Jason decided to look for another job, he pulled out the resume he had used when he applied for the job at Ms. Sensation. Notice how easy it is to find out about Jason.

Jason Cory Kramer
53 Rose Court
Ravine, PA 17966
(717) 555-9682

Objective: To pursue an administrative position that will make use of my communication and organizational skills

Work Experience:

12/9— - Present Office Clerk	Burdick & Modesto, Inc., 807 George Road. Ravine, PA 17966 Did general office work, including word processing, filing, stenography, answering telephones, and making photocopies.
Summer & part time	Independence Insurance, Inc., 193 Campbell Road 199— to 199— Ravine, PA 17966
File Clerk	While in college, worked part-time and summers, filing insurance forms. Also filled in for the receptionist during breaks.

Education:

Ravine Central High School, High School Diploma, 199—
    Major: Business
Downtown Community College, Associate Degree, 199—
    Major: Business Administration

Skills:

Typing (75—80 words per minute); Shorthand (100—120 words per minute); Computer; Dictaphone

References:

Mrs. Violetta Muskin
Office Manager
Independence Insurance, Inc.
193 Campbell Road
Ravine, PA 17966
(717) 555-0200

Mr. Morris Hammel
Instructor
Downtown Community College
83 Placid Street
Ravine, PA 17966
(717) 555-4040

---

1. Suppose you needed to hire an administrative assistant. You received Jason's resume. What facts about Jason would be most important to you?

_____

_____

2. How easy would it be to find the information you were looking for on Jason's resume? Explain your answer.

Check your answers on page 135.

_____

_____

_____

EXERCISE 1 Select Information for a Resume

Before Jason can apply for another job, he will need to update his resume. Help Jason update the experience section of his resume. Look at the list of responsibilities he has at Ms. Sensation. Check off the ones you think are important to include on a resume for an administrative assistant.

_____ a. types

_____ b. does recordkeeping

_____ c. answers the phone

_____ d. handles Steve's correspondence and schedules

_____ e. makes appointments for Steve

_____ f. makes Steve's travel arrangements

_____ g. sorts the mail

_____ h. prepares simple reports

_____ i. keeps Steve informed of the office activities when Steve is out of town

_____ j. brings Steve his morning coffee

_____ k. keeps the office running smoothly during Steve's absences

Check your answers on page 135.

EXERCISE 2 Update the Work Experience Section

Add the responsibilities you chose to the work experience section of Jason's resume. Write the new information on a separate sheet of paper. Be sure to put Jason's most important responsibilities at Ms. Sensation first. Add the ending date for his full-time job at Independence Insurance. Jason left that job in the same month that he began his job at Ms. Sensation. He started working at Ms. Sensation in December 199—, and is still there today. Remember that the address of Ms. Sensation, Inc., is 4891 River Road West in Ravine, Pennsylvania 17966.

Check your answers on page 135.

Workplace Success

EXERCISE 3 Update the Education Section

Check your answers on page 136.

While working at Ms. Sensation, Jason took an evening course at the Ravine Adult Education Center. The course was called "Managing Information on a Computer." It was held between January, 199— and May, 199—. Using a separate sheet of paper, add a listing to the education section of Jason's resume to show this course.

EXERCISE 4 Update the Reference Section

Check your answers on page 136.

Now Jason has more business references he can use. He has decided to take off Mr. Hammel and add Yoli Kroll from Ms. Sensation. Yoli's title is designer. Rewrite the reference section on a separate sheet of paper. Remember to include the correct address. Yoli's phone number at Ms. Sensation is (717) 555-1899.

LESSON 2 Job Applications

When you apply for a job, you are usually asked to fill out a **job application** form. Most forms ask for information similar to that on your resume. But they also ask for some other information. Therefore, it is important to fill out the application form completely. Before you begin, read the entire application. Then fill it in step by step. Although job applications are similar, they are not exactly alike. Therefore, even if you have filled out many applications, you need to read the directions carefully. Pay close attention to the following details:

- Should you put your last name first, or your first name first?
- In what order should you list your previous employers?
- What specific information should you give about your previous jobs and the schools you attended?
- Should you print or use cursive writing?

Example:

Let's look at a real life example of the job application Jason filled out before he was hired at Ms. Sensation. As you look at the application, notice what information it asks for that is not on Jason's resume.

APPLICATION FOR EMPLOYMENT

PERSONAL DATA

NAME	LAST	FIRST	MIDDLE	DATE
	Kramer	Jason	Cory	October 1, 199–

PRESENT ADDRESS (STREET, CITY, STATE, ZIP CODE)
53 Rose Court, Ravine, PA 17966

PERMANENT ADDRESS (IF DIFFERENT FROM ABOVE)

HOME PHONE	BUSINESS PHONE	SOCIAL SECURITY NUMBER	
717-555-9682	717-555-8656	000-00-0000	

EDUCATION

LIST LAST HIGH SCHOOL AND ALL BUSINESS, TRADE SCHOOLS, AND COLLEGES ATTENDED

NAME AND LOCATION OF SCHOOL	MAJOR OR SUBJECTS STUDIED	DEGREE	YEARS ATTENDED
Ravine Central High School	Business	Diploma	199– - 199–
Downtown Community College	Business Administration	Associates Degree	199– - 199–
Ravine Adult Education Center	Computer	—	199–

EMPLOYMENT HISTORY

LIST ALL EMPLOYERS WITH CURRENT OR MOST RECENT EMPLOYMENT FIRST.

PRESENT/LAST EMPLOYER	TELEPHONE NUMBER	SUPERVISOR'S NAME
Ms. Sensation, Inc.	(717) 555-8656	Steven Hart

ADDRESS	DATES EMPLOYED	BASE SALARY OR WAGE
4891 River Road West, Ravine, PA 17966	12/9– TO Present MO. YR. MO. YR.	START $15,000 CURRENT OR END $18,000

POSITION TITLE: Administrative Assistant

SUMMARY OF DUTIES: Typing, filing, record-keeping, office management

REASON FOR LEAVING OR SEEKING CHANGE OF POSITION: Seeking more responsible position

FIRST PREVIOUS EMPLOYER	TELEPHONE NUMBER	SUPERVISOR'S NAME
Burdick & Modesto, Inc.	(717) 555-7906	Violetta Muskin

ADDRESS	DATES EMPLOYED	BASE SALARY OR WAGE
807 George Road, Ravine, PA 17966	12/9– TO 12/9– MO. YR. MO. YR.	START $10,000 CURRENT OR END $12,500

POSITION TITLE: Office Clerk

SUMMARY OF DUTIES: General office work, including word processing, filing, and stenography

REASON FOR LEAVING: Salary was not adequate

NEXT PREVIOUS EMPLOYER	TELEPHONE NUMBER	SUPERVISOR'S NAME
Independence Insurance Company	(717) 555-3000	Albert Wheeler

ADDRESS	DATES EMPLOYED	BASE SALARY OR WAGE
193 Campbell Road, Ravine, PA 17966	6/9– TO 6/9– MO. YR. MO. YR.	START $5.50 / hour CURRENT OR END $5.50 / hr.

POSITION TITLE: File Clerk

SUMMARY OF DUTIES: Fililng, receptionist duties

REASON FOR LEAVING: Part-time, temporary job

MAY WE CONTACT YOUR FORMER EMPLOYER YES ___ NO ✔ PHONE (717) 555-8699

REFERENCES

NAME	TITLE	YEARS ACQUAINTED
Yoli Kroll	Designer	2 years
ADDRESS (STREET, CITY, STATE, ZIP CODE)		TELEPHONE NUMBER
Ms. Sensation, Inc., 4891 River Road West, Ravine, PA 17966		(717) 555-1899
NAME	TITLE	YEARS ACQUAINTED
Violetta Muskin	Office Manager	4 years
ADDRESS (STREET, CITY, STATE, ZIP CODE)		TELEPHONE NUMBER
Independence Insurance, Inc., 193 Campbell Road, Ravine, PA 17966		(717) 555-3000

Jason Kramer
SIGNATURE

10/1/9–
DATE

An Equal Opportunity Employer

Notice that the application asked for Jason's Social Security Number, his past salaries at jobs, reasons for leaving jobs, phone numbers of employers, his business phone number, and both his current and permanent addresses (if they are not the same).

EXERCISE 1 Complete a Job Application

Check your answers on page 136.

Imagine that Jason found another job. He was hired as the administrative assistant to the president of Terrific Women, Inc. This means that his position at Ms. Sensation is open. Suppose you were applying for his position. Fill out the application form on page 93.

APPLICATION FOR EMPLOYMENT

PERSONAL DATA

NAME	LAST	FIRST	MIDDLE	DATE

PRESENT ADDRESS	(STREET, CITY, STATE, ZIP CODE)

PERMANENT ADDRESS	(IF DIFFERENT FROM ABOVE)

HOME PHONE	BUSINESS PHONE	SOCIAL SECURITY NUMBER	

EDUCATION

LIST LAST HIGH SCHOOL AND ALL BUSINESS, TRADE SCHOOLS, AND COLLEGES ATTENDED

NAME AND LOCATION OF SCHOOL	MAJOR OR SUBJECTS STUDIED	DEGREE	YEARS ATTENDED

EMPLOYMENT HISTORY

LIST ALL EMPLOYERS WITH CURRENT OR MOST RECENT EMPLOYMENT FIRST.

PRESENT/LAST EMPLOYER	TELEPHONE NUMBER ( )	SUPERVISOR'S NAME
ADDRESS	DATES EMPLOYED ___/___ TO ___ MO. YR. MO. YR.	BASE SALARY OR WAGE START_____
POSITION TITLE		CURRENT OR END _____

SUMMARY OF DUTIES

REASON FOR LEAVING OR SEEKING CHANGE OF POSITION

FIRST PREVIOUS EMPLOYER	TELEPHONE NUMBER ( )	SUPERVISOR'S NAME
ADDRESS	DATES EMPLOYED ___/___ TO ___/___ MO. YR. MO. YR.	BASE SALARY OR WAGE START_____
POSITION TITLE		CURRENT OR END _____

SUMMARY OF DUTIES

REASON FOR LEAVING

NEXT PREVIOUS EMPLOYER	TELEPHONE NUMBER ( )	SUPERVISOR'S NAME
ADDRESS	DATES EMPLOYED ___/___ TO ___/___ MO. YR. MO. YR.	BASE SALARY OR WAGE START_____
POSITION TITLE		CURRENT OR END _____

SUMMARY OF DUTIES

REASON FOR LEAVING

MAY WE CONTACT YOUR FORMER EMPLOYER   YES ____   NO ____   PHONE ( ) _____

REFERENCES

NAME	TITLE	YEARS ACQUAINTED
ADDRESS (STREET, CITY, STATE, ZIP CODE)		TELEPHONE NUMBER ( )
NAME	TITLE	YEARS ACQUAINTED
ADDRESS (STREET, CITY, STATE, ZIP CODE)		TELEPHONE NUMBER ( )

SIGNATURE   **An Equal Opportunity Employer**   DATE

FOR YOUR Portfolio

WRITE A RESUME

Write a resume you could use if you were applying for a new job. Before you begin, think about your experience, education, and skills. Also select two people to include in the reference section of the resume. You may want to draft your resume below before you prepare a final version below. If possible, type your final resume on a typewriter or word processor.

CHAPTER 10

Reports

On the Job:
Software Company

SOLVING **COMMUNICATION** PROBLEMS

"It's finally launch time," Reggie told Wendall over the phone, "the moment you've been waiting for." He could almost hear Wendall sigh with relief.

"You mean we're finally going to get the new project started?"

"Yep," said Reggie, "I've scheduled a meeting on Friday for the team that will be working on it."

Wendall was the best **programmer** at Infinity, Inc., and Reggie loved having him on his staff. Wendell's ideas were always original. He came up with great solutions before anybody else had even figured out there was a problem. As they spoke now, Reggie was happy that Wendall would be on the team for the new word processing program.

His happiness didn't last, though.

"Friday?" Wendall said, "You expect me to come into the office on *Friday?*"

"Yes, of course," Reggie replied. "You know that was part of the deal for everybody in the **telecommuting** experiment. The company supplies the equipment. You work at home and keep in touch with the office by phone, fax, and e-mail. But everyone comes into the office for meetings."

"Sure," said Wendall, "but that didn't mean *me*."

Reggie sighed. Reggie hadn't been surprised when Wendall volunteered for the telecommuting experiment. Teamwork was not one of Wendell's strengths. He always liked to work alone, and at odd hours. The arrangement had worked well; Wendall always met his **deadlines,** and the quality of his work remained

Words at **WORK**

The following workplace terms are used in this chapter and are defined in the Glossary at the back of this book. If you do not know a word, first try to get the meaning by looking at it in context. Then consider any prefix, suffix, or root. If the meaning is still not clear, look it up in the Glossary.

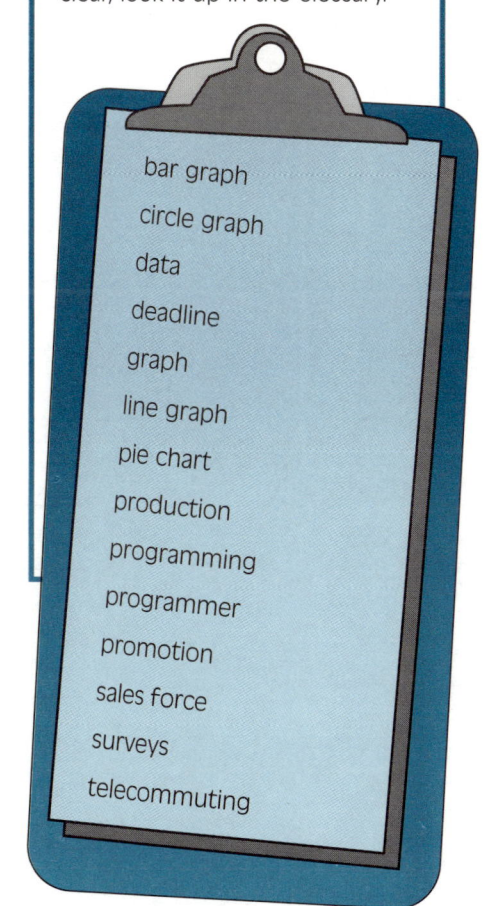

bar graph
circle graph
data
deadline
graph
line graph
pie chart
production
programming
programmer
promotion
sales force
surveys
telecommuting

95

top-notch. Reggie had been able to stop thinking about Wendall and concentrate on supervising the other programmers. Now, however, he needed Wendall in the office.

"Wendall," he said, "I'm afraid you're just going to have to come in Friday. There's no choice."

Wendall sighed. "The meeting is going to be a waste of time," he said. "Why can't I just get started on the project?"

APPLYING **COMMUNICATION** SKILLS

Write your answers to the following questions.

1. What is the main communication problem between Wendall and Reggie?

    _____
    _____
    _____
    _____

2. What might have caused it?

    _____
    _____
    _____
    _____

3. What are some possible solutions to the problem?

    _____
    _____
    _____
    _____
    _____
    _____

4. Select the one solution you think is best. Why would you suggest that Reggie try it?

___

5. If Reggie had to do it over again, what could he have done differently to keep this problem from developing?

___

6. Suppose you were asked to write a set of guidelines for the telecommuting experiment at Infinity, Inc. What kinds of things would you want to cover? Write your ideas on the following lines.

___

Check your answers on page 136.

Workplace Success 97

LESSON 1 Writing Introductory Paragraphs

In a way, a written report is a collection of paragraphs about one main topic. In another way, however, it is much more than that. To begin with, reports usually contain information from many sources. Secondly, the information is put together in an orderly way so that readers can follow it easily. Reports generally contain three parts: the introduction, body, and conclusion. The **introduction,** often a single paragraph, serves two major purposes: It grabs the readers' attention so they want to read on, and it states the topic of the report.

EXAMPLE

Let's look at a real-life introduction from Reggie's report about Infinity, Inc.'s telecommuting experiment.

> Can telecommuting work at Infinity, Inc.? To find the answer to this question, we ran an experimental project that lasted three months. Now that the project is over, it is clear that employees and supervisors were extremely pleased with telecommuting.

1. What did Reggie say to grab the reader's attention?

   _____

   _____

   _____

2. What is the main point that Reggie intends to make in the report itself?

   _____

   _____

Check your answers on page 136.

EXERCISE 1 Set the Stage

Check your answers on page 136.

Suppose Reggie had been asked to write a report telling about the problems with telecommuting. On a separate sheet of paper write an introductory paragraph he could use to open the report.

98   Chapter 10   Reports

LESSON 2 Writing Transitional Paragraphs

You might think of the introductory paragraph of the report as being like the topic sentence of a paragraph. If this is the case, the paragraphs in the **body** are like the supporting sentences. They contain facts, examples, and ideas related to the topic stated in the introduction.

Recall that there are four types of paragraphs: descriptive, narrative, informative, and persuasive. Regardless of the type, paragraphs in a report should be arranged in a logical order. However, sometimes paragraphs need **transitions** to bind them together. By using transitions, you can create bridges from one idea to another. Sometimes a transition can be as simple as a word or phrase at the beginning of one paragraph that shows its relationship to the previous paragraph. For example, you might begin a paragraph with "Another consideration is..." or "Similarly...."

A transitional phrase or sentence will not be enough when moving from one **subtopic** to another. In such cases, you can add a **transitional paragraph**. A transitional paragraph is often no more than two or three sentences. It begins by summarizing the topic that came before and ends by opening the next topic.

EXAMPLE

Let's look at a real-life example of a transitional paragraph.

> Clearly then, telecommuting has many advantages for the employees who work from home. Supervisors also found that having employees telecommute worked out well.

1. What do you think the paragraph that came before the transitional paragraph was about?

   _____

   _____

2. What do you think the paragraph that follows this transitional paragraph is about?

   _____

   _____

Check your answers on page 136.

EXERCISE 1 Bridging the Gap

Read the following paragraphs, then write a transitional paragraph between them.

> Employees with young children like the idea of telecommuting because finding reliable child care can be difficult. With telecommuting, these employees can be at home with their children during the day. They can also schedule their working hours around the times when their children need them most. However, they find they still need help with child care. Otherwise, their work suffers because of interruptions from their children.
>
> _____
>
> _____
>
> _____
>
> _____
>
> _____
>
> _____
>
> _____
>
> _____
>
> Many employees find face-to-face contact with other employees stimulating. They believe that they would not be as creative if they worked alone. Some people even like the trip to and from work. They say it gives them a sense of separation between work and home. Of course, these employees chose not to participate in the telecommuting experiment.

Check your answers on page 136.

LESSON 3 Writing a Conclusion

When you finish writing paragraphs that cover all the facts and ideas that you plan to cover, your report is still not quite complete. You need a concluding paragraph that ties it all together for the reader. The **conclusion** should restate the major topic from the introduction in different words. It should also sum up the main points you made in the body of the report. You can also add an example, a quotation, or a comment that will stick with readers after they finish the report.

EXAMPLE

Let's look at a real life example of a concluding paragraph. It comes from Reggie's report.

> It seems safe to say that just about everyone thought that the experiment was successful. Telecommuting helped employees solve many problems, such as finding child care and commuting every day. For the most part, communications were good, and work quality and output were as high as ever. Of course, there were also problems. However, if Infinity, Inc. decides to let workers continue to telecommute, we can find solutions to these problems. As one supervisor said, "I have an easier time getting in touch with my staff when they're in another county than when they're right down the hall."

1. Compare the paragraph above with the introductory paragraph on page 98. What idea is stated in *both* paragraphs?

   _____
   _____
   _____

2. Based on the concluding paragraph, what important points do you think were made in the body of the report?

   _____
   _____
   _____

Check your answers on page 136.

Workplace Success   101

EXERCISE 1 Tying It All Together

Review the introductory paragraph you wrote about the problems of telecommuting for Exercise 1 on page 98. Suppose the report that followed focused on three problems:

1. Reaching employees when they were needed.
2. Arranging to have employees come into the office when it was necessary.
3. The work of different employees on the same project not blending together.

On a separate sheet of paper write a concluding paragraph that sums up the report.

Check your answers on page 136.

LESSON 4 Illustrating Reports with Tables

Readers can better understand the ideas in a report when they can visualize the information. There are a number of features you can add to a report that will help readers do just that. One such feature is a table. A **table** presents **data** in columns (going down the page) and rows (going across the page).

Tables usually contain the following features:

1. Title
2. Column headings that tell what kind of information the columns contain
3. The columns and rows of information.

Sometimes tables also contain **footnotes** that explain some of the information.

Example:

Let's look at a real-life example of a table that comes from the report Reggie wrote. Reggie got the information for this table from **surveys** of employees and supervisors. Look at the table at the top of page 103 and read the paragraph from the report that goes with it. How does the table help you understand the information?

102 Chapter 10 Reports

> **Table 1. EMPLOYEES FAVORING TELECOMMUTING**
>
> | Department | Percent (%) in Favor |
> |---|---|
> | Human Relations | 30 % |
> | Marketing | 52 % |
> | Promotion | 60 % |
> | Production | 72 % |
> | Programming | 76 % |
> | Sales* | 100 % |
>
> * The sales force spends most of its time on the road and is already communicating electronically with the office.
>
> Six departments were part of the experiment. The opinions about telecommuting varied from department to department. Employees in the **programming** department liked the idea, with 76 percent in favor. **Production** was not far behind, with 72 percent for it. However, only 30 percent of employees in human relations thought telecommuting would work. In the **promotion** department, 60 percent "voted" yes. In the marketing department, 52 percent of the employees said they were for it. The fact that 100 percent of the **sales force** was in favor of telecommuting was not surprising. After all, the sales force now spends almost all its time out on the road, and keeps in touch with the office by e-mail and faxes.

The table leaves out everything except the figures, and it is arranged in logical order. These features make it easy to see how each department reacted and compare their ratings.

EXERCISE 1 Build a Table

Expand Table 1 by adding a title and a second column of data on the percent who would telecommute. Use the information in the following paragraph from Reggie's report.

> Employees were also asked whether they would actually telecommute. We added up the numbers and found that ten percent of the employees in the human relations department said yes. In the marketing department, six percent wanted to telecommute, while 20 percent of the employees in the production department thought they would give it a try. In the programming department, 21 percent of the programmers said they would telecommute. In the promotion department 26 percent said yes, as did 100 percent of the sales force.

Table 1. _____

Department	% in Favor	% Who Would Telecommute
Human Relations	30 %	_____
Marketing	52 %	_____
Promotion	60 %	_____
Production	72 %	_____
Programming	76 %	_____
Sales*	100 %	_____

* The sales force spends most of its time on the road and is already communicating electronically with the office.

Check your answers on page 137.

LESSON 5   Creating Graphs for a Report

Another way to help readers visualize information is with **graphs.** Three common types of graphs are the bar graph, the line graph, and the pie chart, or circle graph.

A **bar graph** is a good way to compare amounts. As the name suggests, bars are used to show quantities. A scale along the side of the graph shows the amounts. By measuring the length of the bars on the scale, readers can find out the amount each one stands for. They can also compare the bars with each other. It's easiest to make a bar graph if you use graph paper.

Line graphs are used to show how something changes over time. Like the bar graph, a line graph has a scale down the side. Instead of using bars to show amounts, dots are placed along a grid. As with bar graphs, it's helpful if you use graph paper.

A **pie chart,** or **circle graph,** compares the parts of a whole. The entire pie, or circle, equals 100 percent. Each "slice" of the pie shows the percentage one part equals. Before you can make a pie chart, you need to figure out the percentage each part you are comparing.

EXAMPLE

Let's look at some real-life examples from Reggie's report.

Figure 10-1 A Bar Graph

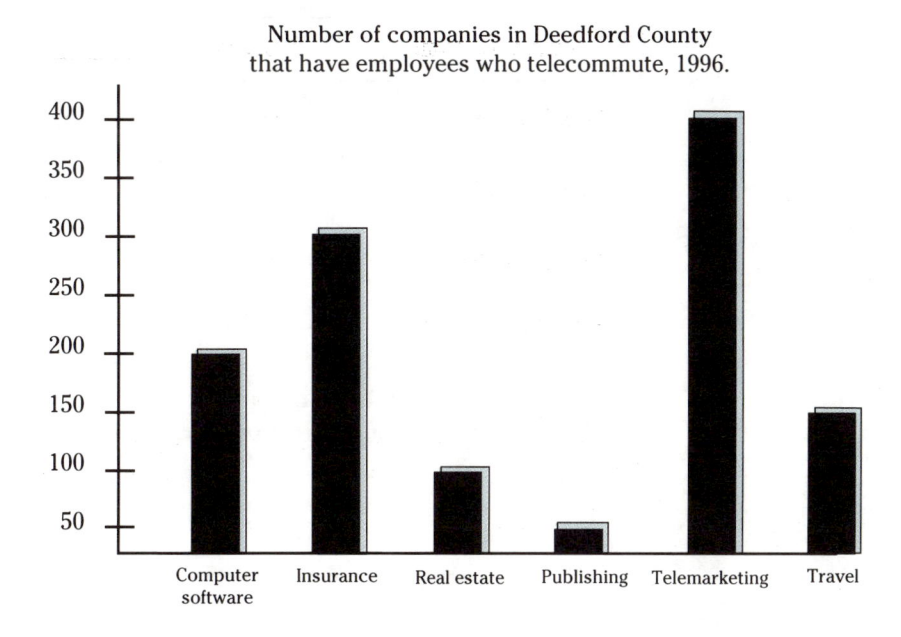

Number of companies in Deedford County that have employees who telecommute, 1996.

Computer software	200
Insurance	300
Real estate	100
Publishing	50
Telemarketing	400
Travel	150

Figure 10-2 A Line Graph

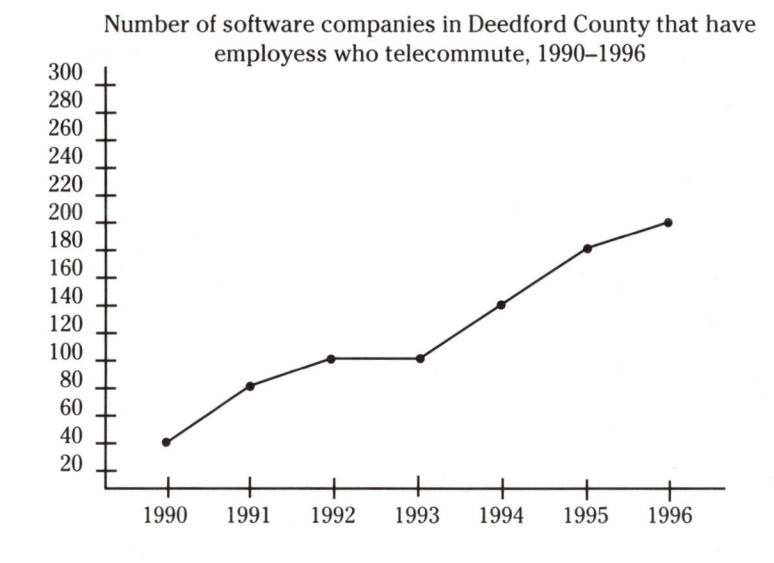

Number of software companies in Deedford County that have employess who telecommute, 1990–1996

Year	Number
1990	40
1991	80
1992	100
1993	100
1994	140
1995	180
1996	200

Figure 10-3 A Circle Graph or Pie Chart

Reasons employees at Infinity, Inc. gave for choosing to telecommute.

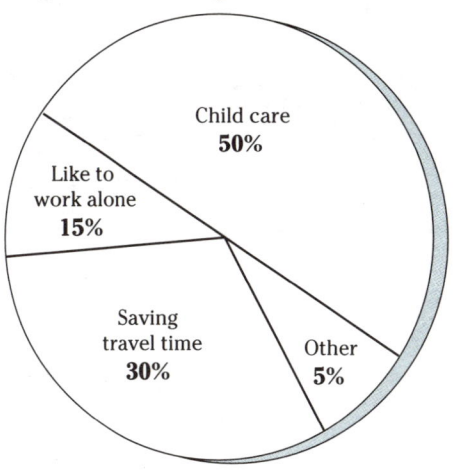

- Child care 50%
- Saving travel time 30%
- Like to work alone 15%
- Other 5%

Workplace Success

1. Could you make a bar graph to show the information in the pie chart? If you could, how would you go about it? If you could not, why not?

   _____

   _____

2. Could you use a circle graph to show the information in the line graph above? If you could, how would you go about it? If you could not, why not?

   _____

   _____

3. Could you use a bar graph to show the information in the line graph? If you could, how would you go about it? If you could not, why not?

   _____

   _____

4. Could you use a line graph to show the information from the bar graph above? If you could, how would you go about it? If you could not, why not?

   _____

   _____

Check your answers on page 137.

EXERCISE 1 Show Information in the Best Way

Decide what kind of graph would be best for showing the information in each item below. Underline your choice.

1. The number of copies of Data-Pro 6 Infinity, Inc., sold every month in 199—.

   bar graph   line graph   circle graph

2. The percent of Infinity, Inc.'s, profits that come from sales of each of its products.

   bar graph   line graph   circle graph

3. The number of work days lost per year between 1985 and 1995 at Infinity, Inc., because of illness.

   bar graph   line graph   circle graph

106   Chapter 10   Reports

Check your answers on page 137.

4. The number of employees in each department at Infinity, Inc., who signed up for the company's training courses.

   bar graph   line graph   circle graph

5. The average number of phone calls that each of the seven customer service representatives handle per day.

   bar graph   line graph   circle graph

EXERCISE 2   Change Tables to Graphs

Use the information from the table on page 103 to make a graph. Choose the type of graph that would best show this information.

Check your answers on page 137.

Workplace Success   107

FOR YOUR Portfolio

COMBINE DIFFERENT KINDS OF PARAGRAPHS

Write a set of guidelines for telecommuting. Start with an introductory paragraph that tells the purpose of the guidelines. Then write at least one paragraph about subtopic 1: the rules telecommuters' should follow. Also write at least one paragraph about subtopic 2: what the supervisors should do. Include a transitional paragraph to create a bridge between the two subtopics. Write a conclusion that sums up the main points. Use additional paper if necessary.

CHAPTER 11

On the Job: Software Company

Revising, Editing, and Proofreading

SOLVING COMMUNICATION PROBLEMS

Reggie picked up the phone and dialed Jeannette's number. "Get in here right away," he told her. "And bring Chandra and Howard with you. We've got a big problem."

While he waited for the team, Reggie began to feel better. If anyone could get him out of this bind, Chandra, Howard, and Jeannette were the ones. They were not only top-notch programmers, but also excellent problem solvers. They wouldn't let go until they got it right.

As soon as the team was seated, Reggie broke the bad news. "I had a call from **customer service.** They've been flooded with complaints from users of Data-Pro 6. It seems there's a giant **bug** on the spreadsheet. I told them we'd have it fixed by Monday. It'll mean working all weekend."

"Why us?" Jeannette asked, "Sandy and Mike had as much to do with Data-Pro as we did. Why don't they have to give up their weekend?"

"Right," said Howard, "I didn't even work on the spreadsheet. Why should Sandy and Mike get to spend the weekend on the beach?"

Reggie sighed. He had thought about including Sandy and Mike, but he knew that they weren't up to the task. It would be wrong to tell that to their coworkers, however.

Words at WORK

The following workplace terms are used in this chapter and are defined in the Glossary at the back of this book. If you do not know a word, first try to get the meaning of it by looking at it in context. Then consider any prefix, suffix, or root. If the meaning is still not clear, look it up in the Glossary.

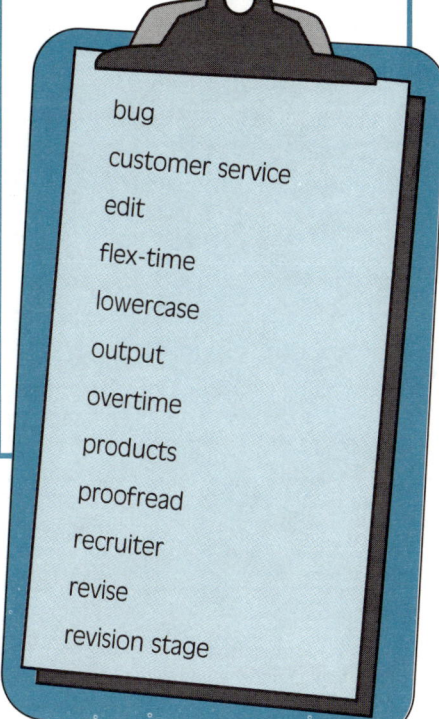

- bug
- customer service
- edit
- flex-time
- lowercase
- output
- overtime
- products
- proofread
- recruiter
- revise
- revision stage

APPLYING **COMMUNICATION** SKILLS

Write your answers to the following questions.

1. What is the main communication problem between Reggie and the three members of his staff?

   _____

   _____

2. What might have caused the problem?

   _____

   _____

3. What are some possible solutions to the problem?

   _____

   _____

   _____

   _____

4. Select the one solution you think is best. Why would you suggest that Reggie try it?

   _____

   _____

   _____

5. How might Reggie change his behavior in the future to keep situations like this from happening again?

   _____

   _____

   _____

Chapter 11 Revising, Editing, and Proofreading

6. Do you think it is ever right for supervisors to ask employees to work weekends and evenings? Jot down your ideas about what the rules for **overtime** should be.

_____
_____
_____
_____
_____
_____
_____

Check your answers on page 137.

LESSON 1   Revising

When you write on the job, it is very important that your words say what you intend them to say, and say it well. You can use the steps in the writing process to help make sure this is the case. When you write the first draft, concentrate on getting your thoughts down on paper. Don't worry about fixing any problems at first. You can correct these problems when you **revise** your draft. In the **revision stage** of the writing process, make sure you have clearly stated all the important points you wanted to make. You can use the revision checklist that follows as a guide. (It's a good idea to put your first draft aside for a few days before you revise it, so that you are fresh when you read it again.)

FYI

REVISION CHECKLIST

1. Did I state my topic clearly so readers will know the main idea?
2. Have I included all the information readers need to know?
3. Did I include only information that is on the topic?
4. Did I arrange the ideas in a logical way?

EXAMPLE

Let's look at a real life example of a paragraph from Reggie's report about the telecommuting experiment. Notice that he double spaced his first draft and wrote the revisions between the lines.

Workplace Success   111

>   Most
> (1) ~~A number of~~ copywriters in the promotion department
> do not like the idea of telecommuting. They
> ^said they missed brainstorming sessions. (2) These sessions
> helped them to come up with good ideas. (3) They also missed
>   and helping each other revise their drafts
> trying out their ideas on other copywriters. (4) ~~One copywriter~~
>   copywriters
> ~~said that teleconferencing might help, but~~ most did not think
> teleconferencing
> ~~that it~~ would be as helpful as face-to-face meetings.

1. Why do you think Reggie changed sentence 1?

   _____

   _____

2. Why do you think Reggie changed sentence 3?

   _____

   _____

Check your answers on page 137.

3. Why do you think Reggie changed sentence 4?

   _____

   _____

EXERCISE 1   Rethink a Paragraph

As you read the paragraph below from Reggie's report on telecommuting, think about ways in which it might be improved. Then answer the questions that follow.

> (1) Clearly, some jobs cannot be done from home. (2) A **recruiter,** for example, needs to be in the office in order to interview job applicants. (3) Recruiters, however, could easily take advantage of **flex-time,** since they could schedule interviews outside of office hours. (4) Most supervisors need to be in the office in case problems arise. (5) The people in the shipping department must, of course, be where the **products** are. (6) For most jobs, however, telecommuting works for at least part of the time.

1. What is the main idea of the paragraph? Is it stated clearly?

   _____

   _____

2. Are all the ideas in the paragraph about the topic? If not, which sentence or sentences should be cut?

   _____

Check your answers on page 137.

3. What purpose might sentence 6 serve in the report?

   _____

   _____

EXERCISE 2 Take a Fresh Look

Check your answers on page 137.

Select any paragraph that you wrote for an earlier chapter of this book. Copy the paragraph on a separate sheet of paper, skipping every other line. Then revise it, using the Revision Checklist on p. 111.

LESSON 2 Editing

The next stage in the writing process is editing. When you **edit,** you try to improve the language you use to express your ideas. At this stage, you should look at words and sentence structure. The editing checklist that follows will help you.

FYI

EDITING CHECKLIST

1. Did I choose words that mean what I intended to say?
2. Did I use specific, rather than general, words?
3. Did I avoid overused words and expressions?
4. Is the tone suitable for my readers?
5. Does each sentence contain a complete idea?
6. Is the meaning of each sentence clear?
7. Are the sentences varied in length and structure?
8. Do all sentences contain a subject and verb?
9. Is the same verb tense used throughout the paragraph?

Workplace Success   113

EXAMPLE

Let's look at a real-life example of editing that Reggie did on a paragraph from his report.

> (1) The community as a whole benefits from telecommuting. Therefore, (2) Rush-hour traffic is decreased, ~~and telecommuting is good for the environment.~~ as is air pollution. (3) Employees do not drive their cars to work on a daily basis. (4) Employees ~~no longer~~ who might otherwise have to spend ~~so much time on the road, so they have more~~ as much as 10 hours a week commuting can use the time ~~to use for other purposes. (5) Many employees choose to use this time~~ in their own communities. (6) They might be likely to spend more time with their children and become ~~more~~ invoved with their children's school. (7) Many also take an active interest in local politics or do volunteer work.

1. Why do you think Reggie changed the last part of sentence 2?

   _____

   _____

2. Why do you think Reggie moved sentence 3?

   _____

   _____

3. Why do you think Reggie changed sentence 4?

   _____

   _____

4. Why do you think Reggie moved part of sentence 5 to sentence 4 and deleted the rest?

   _____

   _____

5. Why do you think Reggie edited sentence 6?

_____

_____

6. Do you think that Reggie's changes make the paragraph clearer? Explain your answer.

_____

_____

_____

_____

Check your answers on page 137.

EXERCISE 1 Find the Flaws

Help Reggie edit the paragraph below by answering the questions that follow it.

> (1) Employees in the telecommuting experiment communicated with the office by telephone, fax, and e-mail. (2) They were instructed to report into the office at least once a day. (3) They were also supposed to keep daily logs, which they send to their supervisors by e-mail once a week. (4) Employees did not have to work 9-to-5. (5) They were expected to be available for at an agreed-upon time during business hours. (6) In other words, if employees wanted to work crazy hours, that was fine, but they also had to make time during the normal business day when people could reach them. (7) In these ways, it was expected that communication with the employees would remain flexible, even though the employees were at home.

1. Are there any words that might not mean what Reggie intended to say? If so, give an example.

_____

_____

2. Are there any general words that Reggie could replace with specific words? If so, give an example.

3. Did Reggie include any overused words and expressions? If so, give an example.

4. Are there any places where the tone does not seem right for readers of a business report? If so, give an example.

5. Are there any sentences that do not contain complete ideas? If so, rewrite the sentence so it contains a complete idea.

6. Are there any sentences that are unclear? If so, give an example. Rewrite the sentence so it is clear.

7. Are there any sentences that do not contain both a subject and a verb? If so, give an example.

8. Are there any sentences that use a verb in a different tense than the tense used in the rest of the paragraph? If so, give an example.

Check your answers on page 138.

EXERCISE 2 Make It Better

Check your answers on page 138.

Copy the revised paragraph from Exercise 2 on page 113 on a separate sheet of paper, skipping lines. Then edit it, using the Editing Checklist on page 113.

LESSON 3 Proofreading

After you have edited a paragraph, you are ready to move on to the proofreading stage of the writing process. When you **proofread** you look for errors in spelling, grammar, and format. Once again, it's a good idea to let some time pass between editing and proofreading. Then force yourself to read word by word, or even letter by letter. Look at every detail. You may want to proofread the paragraph several times, looking for a different type of error each time. Use the proofreading checklist that follows as a guide during this final check.

FYI

PROOFREADING CHECKLIST

1. Did I spell all words correctly? (If you are not certain, look in a dictionary.)
2. Did I capitalize letters where necessary?
3. Did I punctuate sentences correctly?
4. Did I omit any words?
5. Did I accidently repeat any words a second time (*the the*, for example)?
6. Do the subjects and verbs agree in number?
7. Are pronouns in the correct form (*he* or *him*, for example)?
8. Will readers know what noun each pronoun stands for?
9. Are the first lines of paragraphs indented or have I skipped lines between paragraphs?
10. Are margins wide and even?
11. Are any headings positioned and capitalized correctly and consistently?

Example:

Let's look at a real-life example of a paragraph that Reggie has proofread. Think about the types of errors Reggie corrected as you read the paragraph.

PROOFREADING MARKS

- ℛ   delete (take something out)
- ⌒   close up space
- \#   add space
- ∧   insert (add something)
- ⊙   insert (add) a period
- ≡   change a **lowercase** letter to a capital letter
- /   change a capital letter to a lowercase letter

"Supervisors rated the performance of telecommuters on four points; meeting dead lines, communicating with supervisors and coworkers, the quality of their **output,** and the quantity of their output. Most supervisors gave most employees high marks on at least three of the the four points. The area that is most often missing was Communication. It seems many telecommuters did not turn in their reports regularly and were sometimes out of touch when needed. A few employees also let deadlines slip. As one supervisors saidd, "telecommuting is not for everyone. Some employees need the discipline and routine of an office to organize their work lives." It appears, however, many other employees work well when given the freedom to plan they're own days."

---

118   Chapter 11   Revising, Editing, and Proofreading

Did you notice that Reggie corrected errors in spelling, punctuation, and capitalization? He also took out a repeated word, added missing words, corrected the tense of a verb, and added a space where it was needed. Notice how the proofreading marks were used in Reggie's paragraph. The delete mark was used eight times to take out words, letters, and punctuation marks. The caret (^) was used to insert material four times. The space between *dead* and *lines* was closed up. The *C* in *communication* was made lowercase. The *t* in *telecommuting* was capitalized, since it begins a quotation. Space was added just before that quotation.

Use proofreading marks to keep your editing clear.

EXERCISE 1 Hunt for Errors

Proofread the following paragraph from Reggie's report. Make the changes in the space between the lines. Then copy the paragraph on a separate sheet of paper. Remember to keep your margins even.

Check your answers on page 139.

> The experiment met with few technical problems. All telecomuters were lent computers, and some people had trouble setting them up. Break downs were rare, however, and they they seldom had a serious impact the work. Employees who had not work on computers before, found that it took time to earn how to use e-mail. Therefore early in the experiment, they sometimes "lost" their work. however, after this start-up period, the everything went very smothly.

Workplace Success   119

FOR YOUR Portfolio

DRAFT, REVISE, EDIT, AND PROOFREAD A PARAGRAPH

First, on a separate sheet of paper, write a paragraph that states your opinion about supervisors asking employees to work weekends and evenings. When drafting the paragraph, concentrate on the ideas you want to express.

Second, revise the paragraph above to make sure you communicated your ideas clearly and logically.

Third, edit your paragraph to be sure that you used the word and sentence forms that express your ideas well.

Finally, proofread the paragraph for errors in spelling, punctuation, capitalization, and so forth. Use the proofreading checklist as a guide. After you have proofread the paragraph, write the final version on the lines below.

_____

_____

_____

_____

_____

_____

_____

_____

_____

_____

_____

_____

_____

_____

_____

GLOSSARY

Each of the following terms is used in this book. Simple pronunciation guides are shown in slashes following each term. Definitions may expand on those given in the text. Only the use of the word in the book is given here. Any of these words may have additional meanings. Consult a dictionary for more information.

acquisition /ak-KWIH-zih-shuhn/ *noun* The act of buying a company.

admitting office /ad-MIHT-tihng AW-fuhs/ *noun* The department in a retirement home or geriatric facility that processes new residents.

attitude /AT-tuh-tood/ *noun* A way of behaving that shows one's feelings about one's job.

audience /AW-dee-uhns/ *noun* The person or people addressed in a piece of writing.

bar graph /bahr graf/ *noun* A visual method of comparing amounts, using bands of different lengths.

bid /bihd/ *noun* An offer to provide something at a given price.

board /bawrd/ *noun* A group people in an organization that decides the policies.

body /BAHD-ee/ *noun* The part of a piece of writing that contains the core of the information; the part of a letter, or other type of correspondence, that contains the message.

bonus /boh-NUHS/ *noun* A reward, usually of money, for doing a job particularly well.

budget /BUDJ-uht/ *verb* To plan for the spending of money over a specified period.

bug /buhg/ *noun* Something that causes a computer program not to operate correctly.

buyer /BEYE-er/ *noun* A person who purchases goods for a retailer.

buyout /BEYE-owt/ *noun* The act of buying a company.

carbon copy /KAHR-buhn KOHP-ee/ *noun* Originally, a duplicate form created by a sheet of carbon paper or a layer of carbon dust between two pieces of paper. Now used to refer to additional copies of a piece of correspondence sent to people other than the person to whom it is addressed. Abbreviated as cc.

care instructions /kair ihn-STRUHK-shuhns/ *noun* The information that comes with a piece of clothing or other item telling how to maintain it.

Celsius /SEHL-see-uhs/ *adjective* A system of measure for temperature in which water freezes at zero degrees, and boils at 100 degrees.

chain /chayn/ *noun* A number of stores that belong to the same company and that are operated from a single headquarters.

Glossary 121

chronological order /KRAHN-uh-LAHDJ-eh-kuhl OR-der/ *noun* A method of organization based on the order in which things happened.

circle graph /SER-kuhl graf/ *noun* A way of visually comparing parts of a whole by dividing a circle proportionately. Also called *pie chart*.

closing /KLOHZ-ihng/ *noun* The part of a business letter below the body made up of a polite word or phrase and the sender's signature.

clustering /KLUHS-ter-ihng/ *noun* A technique of arranging ideas in visual patterns in order to come up with additional ideas. Also called *mapping*.

commission /kuhm-MIH-shuhn/ *noun* A percentage of each sale given to the salesperson.

comparison and contrast /KUHM-pair-uh-suhn and KAHN-trast/ *noun* A method of organization based on the way two or more things are alike or different.

competition /KAHM-puh-tih-shuhn/ *noun* The rivalry between two or more companies offering the same goods or services.

complaint /kuhm-PLAYNT/ *noun* A form of persuasive writing in which one seeks to have a problem corrected.

concluding sentence /KUHN-kloo-dihng SEHN-tehns/ *noun* A sentence, usually at the end of a paragraph, which summarizes the topic.

conclusion /KUHN-kloo-zhuhn/ *noun* The final part of a report in which the ideas are summarized and tied together.

correspondence /KOR-reh-spahn-duhns/ *noun* Letters, memos, and other means of sending written messages.

coupon /KYOO-pahn/ *noun* A certificate that entitles one to a discount on a specific item or service.

cover sheet /KUHV-er sheet/ *noun* The page of a fax that lists such information as the recipient's and sender's names and fax numbers.

credit /KREHD-iht/ *verb* To restore a sum of money to a credit card or charge account.

customer service /KUST-uh-mer SER-vuhs/ *noun* The facet of a business or organization that relates to dealing with customers' requests and problems.

customer service representative /KUST-uh-mer SER-vuhs rehp-ruh-ZEHNT-tuh-tihv/ noun A person who deals with customers' needs after a purchase.

data /DAYT-uh/ *noun* Information from which a conclusion can be reached.

deadline /DEHD-leyen/ *noun* The date by when something has to be completed.

defective /deh-FEHK-tihv/ *adjective* Faulty; imperfect.

description /DEH-skrihpt-shuhn/ *noun* A form of writing that tells what something is like.

descriptive paragraph /DEH-skrihpt-ihv PAIR-uh-graf/ *noun* A paragraph that tells what something is like.

desktop publishing /DEHSK-tahp PUHB-lih-shihng/ *noun* The production of a document on a computer.

dietitian /DEYE-eht-tih-shuhn/ *noun* A person who specializes in planning healthy diets.

discount /DIHS-kownt/ *noun* An amount deducted from the price of something.

dye /deye/ *noun* A substance used to color cloth, hair, leather, etc.

edit /EHD-eht/ *verb* To make a piece of writing better by improving the expression.

e-mail /EE-mayl/ *noun* Mail sent from one computer to another over phone lines. Also called *electronic mail.*

enclosure /ehn-KLOH-zhuhr/ *noun* A related document sent in the same mailing with a letter. Abbreviated as Enc.

fabric /FAB-rihk/ *noun* The material used to make clothing, draperies, furniture covering, etc.

Fahrenheit /fair-ehn-HEYET/ *noun* A system of measuring temperature in which water freezes at 32 degrees and boils at 212 degrees.

fashion line /FA-shuhn leyen/ *noun* A group of merchandise of the same general class and/or season.

fashion-flair /FA-shuhn-flair/ *noun* A keen sense of what is in style.

flex-time /FLEHKS-teyem/ *noun* A system that permits employees to have individualized work schedules.

food service /food SER-vuhs/ *noun* A company that provides prepared meals to consumers or other companies.

footnote /foot-noht/ *noun* A note at the bottom of a page or table providing additional information or giving sources of information.

form letter /form LEHT-ter/ *noun* A letter with one message sent many people.

format /FOR-mat/ *noun* The way in which something is visually organized.

geriatric /JAIR-ee-at-rihk/ *adjective* Relating to the elderly.

geriatric facility /JAIR-ee-at-rihk FAH-sihl-ih-tee/ *noun* A residence devoted to the elderly and their medical care and physical needs.

graph /graf/ *noun* A visual presentation of data.

greeting /GREET-ihng/ *noun* The part of a business letter above the message made up of the word "Dear" and the title and name of the recipient.

gross /grohs/ *noun* Twelve dozen or 144.

heading /HEHD-ihng/ *noun* The top part of a business letter made up of the address of the sender and the date on which the letter is sent.

headquarters /hehd-KWAWR-terz/ *noun* The main office of an organization.

initiative /ihn-ih-SHAH-tihv/ *noun* The ability to do things without being asked.

inside address /ihn-SEYED AH-drehs/ *noun* The part of a business letter above the greeting that gives the address of the recipient.

introduction /IHN-troh-DUHK-shuhn/ *noun* The first part of a report, which states the main idea and gets the readers' attention.

investment /ihn-VEHST-mehnt/ *noun* The money spent on something in order to earn additional money.

human resources /HYOO-muhn REE-sor-suhs / *noun* The department of a business that involves hiring and dealing with employees, including medical benefits.

job application /jahb AHP-plih-KAY-shuhn/ *noun* The standard form that one fills out when applying for a job.

layoff /lay-AWF/ *noun* The act of dismissing an employee to reduce costs.

line /leyen/ *noun* A series of items for sale, connected by a specific theme.

line graph /leyen graf/ *noun* A method of showing data by placing points on a grid and connecting them with a line.

loan officer /lohn AW-fuh-suhr/ *noun* The person at a bank who arranges loans.

logo /LOH-goh/ *noun* A graphic design depicting a company name or image, used on stationery, its products, and promotional items, such as T-shirts.

lowercase /LOH-er kays/ *adjective* The small form of a letter, as opposed to the capital form.

main idea /mayn eye-DEE-uh/ *noun* The most important point being made about a topic.

mapping /MAP-pihng/ *verb* See *clustering*.

manager /MAN-uh-jer/ *noun* A person who directs and controls an organization.

markdown /MAHRK-down/ *noun* A reduction in price.

maternity leave /muh-TER-neh-tee leev/ *noun* Time granted to a woman to be away from work during childbirth and to care for a newborn baby.

medical insurance /MEHD-ih-kuhl ihn-SHOOR-uhns/ *noun* A system that protects individuals from the costs of illness or accidents.

Medicaid /MEHD-ih-kaid/ *noun* The health insurance plan provided by the Federal government for the elderly in nursing homes.

medication /MEHD-ih-KAY-shuhn/ *noun* Medicine.

memo /MEHM-oh/ *noun* A short note that follows a defined format, usually used to communicate with people within a company.

memory /MEHM-uhr-ee/ *noun* The part of a computer where information is stored.

merchandise /MER-chan-deyes/ *noun* Items intended for sale.

morale /maw-RAL/ *noun* The mood of a person or group of people.

narrative paragraph /NAHR-ruh-tihv PAIR-uh-graf/ *noun* A paragraph that tells about something that happened.

narrative writing /NAHR-ruh-tihv REYE-tihng/ *noun* Writing that tells about something that happened.

niche /nihch/ *noun* The need or position that a company or product fills.

office manager /AW-fuhs MAN-uh-jerr/ *noun* The person at a company who organizes the internal workings of an office.

order form /OR-der form/ *noun* A form for requesting specific goods or services.

order of importance /OR-der uhv ihm-PORT-ehns/ *noun* A method of organization in which details are arranged according to their importance.

outline /OWT-leyen/ *noun* A structured list showing the topics and subtopics of a paragraph or report.

output /OWT-put/ *noun* The amount made or done within a specific time.

overtime /OH-vehr-teyem/ *noun* Extra time spent working.

paragraph /PAIR-uh-graf/ *noun* A group of sentences that develop a single idea.

paternity leave /pah-TER-nuh-tee leev/ *noun* Time granted to a man to be away from work to care for a newborn baby.

persuasive writing /per-SWAY-sihv REYET-ihng/ *noun* Writing intended to convince the reader to do or think something.

performance appraisal /per-FAWR-muhnts uh-PRAY-zehl/ *noun* The evaluation of an employee's work.

physical therapy /FIHS-ih-kuhl THAIR-uh-pee/ *noun* The treatment of a disease or injury by physical means, as with exercises or massage.

pie chart /peye chahrt/ *noun*   A way of visually comparing parts of a whole by dividing a circle proportionately. Also called *circle graph*.

procedures /PROH-see-jerz/ *noun*   A way of doing a particular job, such as processing a sales order.

production /PROH-duhk-shuhn/ *noun*   The act of making a product.

productivity /PROH-duhk-TIHV-eh-tee/ *noun*   The rate at which goods are produced.

products /PRAH-duhkts/ *noun*   The items for sale.

profit center /PRAH-fiht SEHN-ter/ *noun*   A department of a business that is expected to earn money.

programmer /PROH-gram-ehr/ *noun*   A person who designs a computer program.

programming /PROH-grahm-ihng/ *noun*   The act of creating computer programs.

promotion /PRUH-moh-shuhn/ *noun*   A department within a organization which utilizes advertising, publicity, or discounts (such as coupons) to encourage the sale of a product and customer preference for the organization.

proofread /PROOF-reed/ *verb*   To check a piece of writing for errors.

purchase order /PUHR-chuhs OR-der/ *noun*   A form for placing an order to buy something.

purpose /PER-puhs/ *noun*   The reason for writing a paragraph or document.

qualifications /KWAL-ih-fih-KAY-shuhn/ *noun*   The skills, training, experience, and education that fits a person for a specific job.

recognition /reh-KUHG-nih-shuhn/ *noun*   The act of taking notice of or showing approval of.

recreational therapy /rehk-REE-aye-shuhn-uhl THAIR-uh-pee/ *noun*   The use of amusement and relaxation to treat a condition.

recruiter /ree-KROO-ter/ *noun*   A person who seeks and screens people to fill jobs.

reference /REHF-er-ehns/ *noun*   A person who can vouch for the qualifications of a job applicant.

reimburse /REE-ihm-bers/ *verb*   To pay back money that has been spent.

resume /REHZ-uh-may/ *noun*   A document that summarizes a job hunter's qualifications.

retail /REE-tayl/ *noun*   The selling of goods directly to the people who will use them.

retirement home /ruh-TEYE-er-mehnt hohm/ *noun*   An apartment building or complex that is dedicated to retired senior citizens. It includes medical care and recreational activities.

revenue /REHV-ehn-yoo/ *noun* Money taken in by a business.

revise /REE-veyez/ *verb* To make a piece of writing better by improving the way ideas are expressed.

revision /REE-vih-shuhn/ *noun* The form or a piece of writing that results from revising; the act of revising.

salary /SAL-uh-ree/ *noun* A fixed amount of money paid, on a weekly or biweekly basis, to an employee by the organization.

sales force /saylz fawrs/ *noun* The group of people who sell a product or service.

screen /skreen/ *verb* The part of a computer monitor where information is displayed.

self appraisal /sehlf uh-PRAY-zehl/ *noun* An employee's evaluation of his or her performance at work.

sequential order /SEE-kwehn-shuhl OR-der/ *noun* A method of organization in which details are arranged so that they follow each other in a systematic way, such as alphabetically or numerically.

signature /SIHG-nah-cher/ *noun* The part of the closing of a business letter made up of the sender's typewritten and handwritten name.

social worker /SOH-shuhl WERK-er/ *noun* A person who works to help people cope in a community or organization.

spatial order /SPAYE-shuhl OR-duhr/ *noun* A method of organization in which details are arranged according the their position in space.

spreadsheet /SPREHD-sheet/ *noun* A computer program that provides a worksheet with rows and columns to be used for calculations.

standard procedure /STAHND-duhrd proh-SEE-juhr/ *noun* A fixed method of operation.

stock /stohk/ *noun* The amount of goods kept on hand for sale.

subtopic /suhb-TAHP-ihk/ *noun* A secondary subject covered within a topic.

supplier /suh-PLEYE-er/ *noun* An organization or person who provides goods or services.

supporting sentence /suh-POR-tihng SEHN-tehns/ *noun* A sentence that explains or develops the main idea.

surger /SER-jer/ *noun* An industrial sewing machine.

table /TAY-buhl/ *noun* A display of data in columns and rows.

telecommuting /TEHL-eh-KAHM-myoo-tihng/ *noun* The act of working away from an office, and keeping in touch by electronic means such as e-mail, fax, and telephone.

tone /tohn/ *noun* The way something is said. Tone expresses emotions.

topic /TAH-pihk/ *noun* The general subject of a piece of writing.

topic sentence /TAH-pihk SEN-tehns/ *noun* The one sentence that summarizes the main idea of a paragraph.

trade association /trayd uh-SOH-see-aye-shuhn/ *noun* An organization made up of companies or people that share a business interest.

transition /TRANZ-ih-shuhn/ *noun* A bridge between ideas.

transitional paragraph /TRANZ-ih-shuhn-uhl PAIR-uh-graf/ *noun* A paragraph that serves as a bridge between two ideas.

unity /YOO-nih-tee/ *noun* The effect created when all the parts of a paragraph work together.

venture /VEHN-cher/ *noun* A business investment in which there is a risk of losing money.

warranty /WAR-uhn-tee/ *noun* A promise, in writing, from a manufacturer assuring that a product will be repaired or replaced if it malfunctions, within a specified period of time, at no cost to the customer.

workstations /werk-STAY-shuhns/ *noun* The furniture and equipment at which an employee works.

ANSWER KEY

CHAPTER 1

APPLYING COMMUNICATION SKILLS

1. Darlene's main communication problem is that she did not want to write a self appraisal as part of her annual performance appraisal.

2. Darlene did not understand why writing her self appraisal was necessary. She also seemed not to know that this was standard procedure at Peachtree Fashion Stores. She wants her boss to make an exception to the rule because she is not good at writing.

3. Some possible solutions to the problem include:
   - Darlene could quit before her self appraisal is due.
   - She could ask again for an exception to the writing rule and try to just discuss her performance.
   - Darlene could ask a friend or relative for help in writing her self appraisal now and then look for more help in learning to write later.

4. The last solution given above is the best choice because it meets both her short-term and long-term needs.

5. Suggested answer: Darlene could look for adult education courses in writing in her community.

6. Answers will vary.

LESSON 1

Example
1. Jim is writing to Sara White.
2. Jim is writing because his phone is broken and must be fixed. His boss told him to write to Sara.
3. The deadline for the task is May 3.
4. Suggested answer: Jim's memo contains important information but is not tactful.
5. Jim stated these things well: the exact nature of problem, time it started, and when he needs it fixed and why.
6. Jim's request for quick repair was not tactful. His extension number belongs in the Subject line. He did not give Jill's last name or extension. Also, Sara may get annoyed at being told what her job is and being told to "fix it fast," which implies that she usually takes her time.

Exercise 1
1. c
2. d
3. a
4. d

Exercise 2
Main Idea: My office phone gets no dial tone. I need it repaired quickly.

Supporting Details: Answers will vary. A sample answer follows.

1. It broke at 11 AM.
2. I can be reached at Tom Brown's phone, ext. 2205.
3. I have a rush job due in two days so I need my phone fixed as soon as possible.

LESSON 2

Exercise 1
A. Topic sentence 1   conclusion 5
B. Topic sentence 1   conclusion 4
C. Topic sentence 1   conclusion 4
D. Topic sentence 2   conclusion 4

CHAPTER 2

APPLYING COMMUNICATION SKILLS

1. Darlene and Rosie have different ideas about what's fair in terms of sharing the customers who come into the store.

2. Rosie might be jealous because Darlene is a more capable salesperson. Rosie might wait on more than her fair share of customers. Rosie might not have realized that Mrs. Paracha was one of Darlene's regular customers. Rosie may be anxious to make more money.

3. Possible answers include:
   - Darlene and Rosie could agree to share customers equally.
   - Darlene could make it clear to Rosie that certain customers are hers, and Rosie could stay away from those customers.
   - Darlene could "give" some of her customers to Rosie.
   - Darlene could agree to help Rosie improve her selling skills so that she, too, could develop a set of regular customers.

4. Answers will vary. The fourth solution listed above is best. Most people will agree that Darlene should help Rosie establish regular customers. By doing so, Darlene will also help the store become more successful, and in the long run, help herself.

5. Answers will vary. It was mentioned that Darlene was good at helping customers find exactly what they want. Therefore, it is likely that she pays more attention to what customers say and makes a point to remember their likes and dislikes.

Answer Key   129

LESSON 1

Example
1. The purpose of paragraph 1 is to compare this year's sale with last year's sale.
2. The purpose of paragraph 2 is to explain how to ring up sale items.
3. Paragraph 1 gives information about the features of this year's sale and last year's sale. Paragraph 2 gives specific instructions about how purchases made in this year's sale should be handled by salespeople.

Exercise 1
The following items should be checked.
Items that show sales and profit growth over time: 2, 6, 7
Items that show increased workload: 1, 4, 5, 8

Exercise 2
Answers will vary, but the paragraph should include the points checked in Exercise 1.

LESSON 2

Example
1. The audience for paragraph 1 is customers.
2. The audience for paragraph 2 is the manufacturer.
3. The tone of paragraph 1 is softer and more friendly than the tone of example 2.

Exercise 1
1. F 5. F
2. C 6. F
3. C 7. C, M, F
4. M 8. C, M

Exercise 2
Answers will vary, but should be written in a tone that is appropriate for addressing a customer and should include facts that would appeal to the particular type of customer.

Exercise 3
Answers will vary. The paragraph should state only the facts about the incident, in a businesslike tone.

LESSON 3

Example
1. The topic of this paragraph is the new evening hours at Peachtree Fashions.
2. The topic sentence is: "Starting October 15th, Peachtree Fashions will be open late two evenings a week."
3. The purpose of this paragraph is to announce the new store hours.
4. The audience for the paragraph is Peachtree Fashions' customers.

Exercise 1
Answers will vary but should state that a new employee will be starting work at Peachtree Fashions. Sample answer: I am pleased to announce that a new salesperson, Jennifer Kendra, will be joining the staff.

Exercise 2
Answers will vary. Sample answer: We need to hire a new salesperson to serve our growing number of customers and to continue our growth in profits.

Exercise 3
Answers will vary. Paragraphs should begin with a topic sentence announcing the sale and the preview days. Other sentences should give information about the event. The tone should be friendly.

CHAPTER 3

APPLYING COMMUNICATIONS SKILLS

1. Mei-Mei did not know that Mr. Horton wanted the specials copied on blue paper.
2. As a regular customer, Mr. Horton took it for granted that everybody in the shop knew that he wanted blue paper, so he was careless about filling out his order form.
3. Possible answers include:
   - Jamilla can offer to copy the specials over for free.
   - She can tell Mr. Horton that she will do the copies over immediately, but he will have to pay for the new ones.
   - She can tell Mr. Horton that it was his mistake, and if he is going to yell at the people who work in her shop, she will be happy to see him take his business elsewhere.
4. Answers will vary. The first solution listed above is best. Most people will think that Jamilla should redo the copies at no charge because Mr. Horton is a good customer. Even though this solution will cost Jamilla money, it will keep an important customer from going elsewhere.
5. Answer will vary. Most people will agree that she should reassure Mei-Mei that she did not do anything wrong, but also explain to her that "the customer is always right."
6. Answers will vary.

LESSON 1

Exercise 1
Answers will vary. They might include connections to the community, better service, knowing the customers personally.

Exercise 2
Answers will vary. They might include such things as small stationery items, greeting cards, and fancy papers.

LESSON 2
Example
1. The computer training idea grew out of "computer services."
2. The ideas that grew out of computer training were word processing, desktop publishing, and spreadsheets.

Exercise 1
Answers will vary.

Exercise 2
Answers will vary.

LESSON 3
Example
1. Ideas 1 and 2 offer reduced prices.
2. Ideas 3 and 4 are ways to spread the word about Clear & Quick.
3. Ideas 5, 6, and 7 are ways of bringing people into the store.

Exercise 1
1. Comparison and contrast
2. Chronological
3. Chronological
4. Spatial
5. Order of importance
6. Order of importance
7. Order of importance (or sequential order)
8. Sequential order

Exercise 2
Answers will vary.

Exercise 3
Answers will vary.

CHAPTER 4
APPLYING COMMUNICATIONS SKILLS
1. Mei-Mei thinks that Jamilla promised a bonus to the person who came up with the best idea for saving the business, but Jamilla doesn't remember making that promise.
2. Possible answers: Jamilla might have been so carried away at the meeting where she asked her staff for ideas that she made the promise without thinking about it; or Mei-Mei might have misunderstood something that Jamilla said.
3. Possible answers include:
   - Jamilla can give Mei-Mei a bonus now, and try to pretend that she had always intended to.
   - Jamilla can tell Mei-Mei she is sorry Mei-Mei is upset, and explain that Mei-Mei must have misunderstood her.
   - Jamilla can take every opportunity in the future to reward her staff members and keep them informed about how the business is doing.
4. Answers will vary. The third solution listed above may be best. Most people will agree that Jamilla cannot change what she has done in the past, but can work to renew Mei-Mei's trust and rebuild morale in the future.
5. Answers will vary. Rewards might include bonuses, letters of commendation, being given a medal or certificate, an "employee of the month" program, and so forth.

LESSON 1
Example
1. The topic is opening a new coffee bar at Clear & Quick.
2. Mei-Mei probably points out that the coffee bar will attract customers and that Clear & Quick will earn more profits from it.

Exercise 1
1. We want to make your time at Clear & Quick as pleasant as possible. Therefore, we would like you to help yourself to a free cup of coffee while you wait.
2. Whatever it is, special efforts deserve recognition. So from now on, I am going to honor one outstanding employee every month.
3. Clearly, Mei-Mei is making an extra effort to help Clear & Quick succeed.

Exercise 2
1. b
2. a

Exercise 3
Answers will vary, but will stress that Mr. Horton's business will benefit from coffee bar.

Exercise 4
Answers will vary.

LESSON 2
Exercise 1
3, 4

Exercise 2
Items 1, 2, 3, 4, and 7 should be checked.

Exercise 3
Answers will vary. The paragraph should start with a topic sentence, include supporting sentences about the details in Exercise 2, items 1, 2, 3, 4, and 7, and end with a concluding sentence.

CHAPTER 5

APPLYING COMMUNICATION SKILLS

1. Mr. Demasi's nephew does not understand why Alberto objects to his taking Mr. Demasi off the grounds without informing the staff.
2. The nephew does not know or agree the rules at Sunset House; because Alberto was upset, he was not tactful when confronting the nephew about the rules.
3. Possible answers include:
   - Alberto could ask the social worker to talk to Mr. Demasi and his uncle about following the rules.
   - When he isn't upset, Alberto could talk to Mr. Demasi's nephew again.
   - Alberto could report Mr. Demasi's nephew to the director of Sunset House.
4. The first solution listed above is best. Alberto should ask Susan Long to speak to Mr. Demasi and his nephew about the rules. Social workers are trained to handle problems among staff, relatives, and residents.
5. Written guidelines give rules and the reasons for them. If there were written guidelines, Mr. Demasi, his nephew, and Alberto would be able to refer to them. Alberto would then not risk getting into an argument over a subject he cannot control.
6. Answers will vary.

LESSON 1

Example
1. The topic of the paragraph is procedures for welcoming new residents. The first sentence states this topic.
2. They are arranged in chronological order.
3. Word clues are *to start, before, while,* and *after.*

Exercise 1
a. 1   b. 3   c. 5   d. 2   e. 4

Exercise 2
Answers will vary.

LESSON 2

Example
1. Paragraph one.
2. Answers will vary. Sample answer: brick mansion, quiet country estate, 50 private rooms, comfortable furniture, modern wing, state-of-the-art medical facilities.

Exercise 1
Answers will vary.

Exercise 2
1. b   2. a   3. b   4. a

Exercise 3
Answers will vary.

LESSON 3

Example
1. Mrs. Wong was involved.
2. Mrs. Wong increased her strength.
3. It happened at Sunset House.
4. It happened over a three-month period beginning last October.
5. She was given physical therapy.

Exercise 1
Answers will vary.

CHAPTER 6

APPLYING COMMUNICATIONS SKILLS

1. Melanie and Herman have different ideas about the conversation that took place when Melanie first ordered the thermometers.
2. Melanie might not have spoken clearly when she placed the order. Herman might have made a mistake when he wrote up the order.
3. Possible answers include:
   - Melanie can accept Herman's conditions and agree to pay the extra shipping charges.
   - Melanie can insist that she not have to pay the charges since the problem wasn't her fault.
   - Melanie can suggest that they split the difference.
4. The third solution listed above is best. Splitting the difference is the best choice, since she and Herman have worked together successfully in the past, and she probably will want to continue to deal with Ace.
5. Melanie might place all orders in writing, or if she telephones in an order, follow up with a written or faxed purchase order.
6. Answers will vary.

LESSON 1

Example
1. The purpose is to encourage Sunset House to hire the writer as a nursing assistant.
2. The writer worked at Memorial Hospital; his or her patients there included the elderly, he or she assisted in many different kinds of medical procedures, and dealt with patients, the staff, and patients' families.

3. He or she has never worked at a geriatric facility before.
4. He or she explains that he or she has worked with many elderly patients.

Exercise 1
1. p
2. o
3. x
4. p
5. p
6. p
7. p
8. x
9. o
10. p
11. p
12. p
13. x
14. p
15. p

Exercise 2
Answers will vary.

LESSON 2
Example
1. Mr. Demasi's nephew has not submitted Medicaid forms for his uncle.
2. Sunset house will not be reimbursed by Medicaid until it has the forms.
3. The writer is asking the reader to submit the forms immediately.

Exercise 1
1. The pressure control on the whirlpool is not working.
2. The pressure is adjusted differently for different residents.
3. The reader should repair or replace the whirlpool bath, as promised by the warranty.

Exercise 2
Answers will vary.

LESSON 3
Exercise 1
1. The pressure control on the whirlpool is not working, and the Relaxercise Corporation has not fixed or replaced it.
2. Sunset House is unable to use the whirlpool bath.
3. Repair or replace the whirlpool bath, as promised by the warranty.
4. Answers will vary. If Sunset House has not yet paid for the whirlpool bath, you could threaten not to do so (and to return the bath). Otherwise, you could threaten to report the matter to a trade association or governmental agency.

Exercise 2
Answers will vary.

CHAPTER 7
APPLYING COMMUNICATION SKILLS
1. Yoli and Steve have different ideas about what matters to the business.
2. They see the business from their different perspectives, and do not understand each other's problems or needs.
3. Possible answers include:
   - Yoli and Steve can stop dealing with each other directly and only communicate through Jason.
   - Yoli and Steve can try to explain to each other what their jobs entail and why they have the concerns they do.
   - Jason can ask Steve to write memos of this kind in the future instead of asking Yoli to do it.
   - Yoli can go back to school and take some business courses so that she can give Steve the kind of information he wants.
4. Answers will vary. The second solution listed above is the best. Most people will agree that Steve and Yoli should talk over their problem and help each other understand their points of view.
5. Answers will vary. Most people might think that problem-solving and planning teams would reflect a wide range of points of views. Team members would become more knowledgeable about the overall workings of the company, and thereby become better at their jobs. Most people might think that if Yoli and Steve had been on such teams, they would have understood each other better.

LESSON 1
Exercise 1
The top of the memo should read as follows:

To: Libby Cadley
From: Jason Kramer
Date: August 20, 199—
Subject: Reserving Conference Room (wording may vary).

The message will vary. It should contain the fact that Steve wants to reserve the conference room, and give the time and date that he needs it. It can be as short as one sentence.

Answer Key 133

LESSON 2

Example
1. a. B   b. B   c. F   d. B   e. B   f. F
2. Subject line. (e)
3. Fax number (c) and number of pages (f).

Exercise 1
The subject and message sections should be filled in. Some people may assume that they need to fill in the "To" line. Actually, the sender chooses the name from a list in the computer's memory. Wording of the subject and message sections may vary, but should include the information about the availability of the spandex.

Exercise 2
From: Rita Rodriguez
To: Yoli Kroll
Time: 11:15 AM
Date: September 20, 199—
Subject: Availability of spandex fabric (Wording may vary but should match Exercise 1.)
Message: Wording of the message should be the same as the message in Exercise 1.

Exercise 3
Date: September 20, 199—
To: Rita Rodriguez
Fax: (717) 555-1945
From: Yoli Kroll
Fax: (717) 555-1842
Phone: (717) 555-1899
Number of pages (including cover sheet): 1
Message: Wording of messages will vary, but should include the amounts of each color of spandex Yoli wants reserved and the amount of silver spandex she wants to order.

LESSON 3

Example
1. Yoli telephoned first.
2. She wanted him to return her call.
3. She wanted to know if he had set up the meeting yet.
4. Mr. Longo will be out of the office most of the afternoon and won't be able to receive calls. Therefore, he will call Steve again.
5. He knows that Steve has all this information.
6. Since Yoli is using a phone within the company, only her telephone extension is necessary.

Exercise 1
The form should include the following information. Wording of the message may vary.
To: Yoli Kroll
Date: 8/15/9—
Time: 4:30
M: Mr. Steve Hart
Tel. No: X899
_X_   Telephone
_X_   Message (below)

Messages may vary but should say that Steve called to say that the meeting with Mr. Longo of the bank is set for 10 AM on August 23.
Sally Drumm

CHAPTER 8

APPLYING COMMUNICATION SKILLS

1. Yoli thinks Jason should defend her more with Steve, but Jason does not feel he can express his views to his boss.
2. Yoli does not understand the nature of the supervisor/employee relationship that Jason and Steve have.
3. Possible answers include:
   - Jason could do what Yoli asks, and defend her to Steve.
   - Jason could explain further to Yoli why he cannot defend her to Steve.
   - Jason can tell Yoli that if she thinks friendship requires risking his job, then they can't be friends anymore.
4. Answers will vary. The second solution listed above is best. Most people will think that Jason should try to explain to Yoli why he cannot do more to defend her to Steve.
5. Answers will vary.

LESSON 1

Example
1. The heading appears on the right side of the paper.
2. The name and title of the person who will receive the letter is also in the inside address.
3. The company name and address is printed on the stationary, so it is not repeated in the heading.

Exercise 1
The heading will vary, but should follow the standard business letter format including the sender's address

and the date. The inside address and greeting should read:

    Human Relations Department

    Ms. Sensation, Inc.

    4891 River Road West

    Ravine, PA 17966

    Dear Human Resources Department:
    (or To whom it may concern:)

LESSON 2
Example
1. Steve Hart's title is president. It is part of the closing.
2. Yoli Kroll will receive a copy. Her name is listed after "cc:"
3. Specifications for model 21346 surger will be sent with the letter. It says so after "Enc.:"

Exercise 1
Closings will vary. Signatures should be followed by either "Enclosure" or "Enc." Listing the enclosures is optional.

LESSON 3
Example
1. The inside address is the same as the recipient's address on the envelope.
2. The company name and address would be typed in the upper left-hand corner.

Exercise 1
Return addresses will vary. The address should read:

    Human Resources Department

    Ms. Sensation, Inc.

    4891 River Road West

    Ravine, PA 17966

LESSON 4
Exercise 1
The following inside address and greeting should be added:

    Mr. Leroy Benning

    Vice President

    Tucker Supplies, Inc.

    53 Market Street

    Ravine, PA 17966

    Dear Mr. Benning:

"Tucker Supplies, Inc." should be inserted in the blank in the letter.

CHAPTER 9
APPLYING COMMUNICATION SKILLS
1. Jason thinks that Steve has been purposely keeping information from him so he will not find out that Steve plans to sell the company.
2. Steve might be afraid that if he lets Jason know what is going on, Jason will pass the information on to other employees. Or Jason may be jumping to a wrong conclusion.
3. Possible answers include:
   - Jason can confront Steve to find out whether it is true that the company might be sold.
   - Jason can talk to Steve about his lack of trust, and assure him that he always keeps confidential information to himself.
   - Jason can ask Steve whether it is true that the company might be sold.
   - Jason can take advantage of the access he has to Steve's files and try to find the information on his own.
   - Jason can quit his job, not only because the company is being sold, but also because he thinks Steve does not trust him.
   - Jason can talk to other employees to find out if they know anything about a possible acquisition.
4. Answers will vary. The second solution listed above is best. Most students will agree that Jason should talk to Steve about the problem. The conclusion that Jason has reached may not be correct. Not only that, even if the company is going to be sold, Jason still might not lose his job.
5. Answers will vary.

LESSON 1
Example
1. Answers will vary. Most people will agree that the business skills and range of office tasks he has handled in past jobs would be most important.
2. It would be very easy. The resume is organized so that you can quickly see what he has done at each job, and what business skills he has.

Exercise 1
Answers may vary. Most people will choose from among these items: a, b, d, e, f, h, i, *and* k.

Exercise 2
Wording of the new entry will vary, but should include responsibilities chosen in Exercise 1. The dates for his job at Ms. Sensation should be 12/9— to Present. It should be listed first in the experience section.

Exercise 3
The new entry should read, 1/199— - 5/199—, Ravine Adult Education Center, "Managing Information on a Computer." *It should be listed first in the education section.*

Exercise 4
The new entry should read: Yoli Kroll, Designer, Ms. Sensations, Inc., 4891 River Road West, Ravine, PA 17966 (717) 555-1899
The order of entries can vary.

LESSON 2
Exercise 1
Answers will vary, but all items should be filled in completely.

CHAPTER 10

APPLYING COMMUNICATION SKILLS

1. Wendall doesn't want to come into the office for a staff meeting. He doesn't accept the fact that Reggie is in a position to tell him what he has to do.
2. Teamwork is not one of Wendell's strengths. By letting him work at home, Reggie has reinforced Wendell's reluctance to work with others.
3. Possible answers include:
   - Reggie can tell Wendall that he has to show up at the meeting if he wants to keep his job and his work-at-home arrangement.
   - Reggie can tell Wendall that he won't be able to work on the project unless he's at the meeting.
   - Reggie can let Wendall skip the meeting.
   - Reggie can reschedule the meeting for a more convenient day.
   - Reggie can do either of the last two things, but also make it clear that from now on, Wendall needs to be available during office hours from time to time, even though he's working mainly at home.
4. Answers will vary. The fourth solution listed above is best. Reggie might reschedule the meeting for a more convenient day, as long as he makes it clear to Wendall that he's expected to attend meetings any day of the week in the future. Reggie doesn't want to lose Wendall as an employee, so he wouldn't want to fire him or do anything that would lead him to quit. On the other hand, he needs to make sure that Wendall understands that he is subject to the same rules as everybody else.
5. Answers will vary. Possible answers include:
   - He could have made a point to have more frequent contacts with Wendall.
   - He could have supervised Wendall more closely.
   - He could have had Wendall come into the office more often.
6. Answers will vary. Possible answers include working regular hours, meetings, scheduling assignments, and reporting methods.

LESSON 1
Example
1. He asked the question, "Can telecommuting work at Infinity Inc.?"
2. Supervisors and employees reacted enthusiastically to the project.

Exercise 1
Answers will vary, but will state the topic of the paragraph succinctly and contain an attention-getter.

LESSON 2
Example
1. The paragraph before the transitional paragraph was about the advantages of telecommuting to employees who work at home.
2. The paragraph that follows the transitional paragraph is about the advantages of telecommuting to supervisors.

Exercise 1
Answers will vary, but the transitional paragraph should link the subtopic of why some workers want to telecommute and the subtopic of why some workers choose not to telecommute.

LESSON 3
Example
1. Reactions to the experiment were positive.
2. Telecommuting solved problems for employees. It did not decrease communications, quality, or output. The problems that came up can be solved.

Exercise 1
Answers will vary but should restate the topic (problems with telecommuting) and summarize the main points the writer wants to make about the three problems (reaching employees, arranging to have employees come to the office, and having the work of different employees on the same project blend together).

LESSON 4

Exercise 1

Table 1. **Employees Favoring Telecommuting and Employees who would Choose to Telecommute**

Department	% in Favor	% Who Would Telecommute
Human Relations	30 %	10 %
Marketing	52 %	6 %
Promotion	60 %	26 %
Production	72 %	20 %
Programming	76 %	21 %
Sales*	100 %	100 %

*The sales force spends most of its time on the road, and is already communicating electronically with the office.

LESSON 5

Example
1. Yes. Each bar would be a reason for telecommuting.
2. No. The information does not have to do with parts of a whole.
3. Yes. You would have one bar for each year.
4. No. This graph does not show how things change over time.

Exercise 1
1. Line graph
2. A circle graph is best, but a bar graph could also be used.
3. Line graph
4. Bar graph
5. Bar graph

Exercise 2
The only type of graph that will work for the information is a bar graph. Graphs will vary.

CHAPTER 11

APPLYING COMMUNICATION SKILLS

1. Reggie has asked these three staff members to work over the weekend on an emergency project. The staff members don't understand why they've been chosen and think they're being punished.
2. Reggie neglected to tell them that he didn't think the people responsible for creating the problem were up to the take and that he was asking his team because he thinks so highly of them.
3. Possible answers include:
   - Reggie can get Sandy and Mike to help, too.
   - Reggie can tell them that they don't have to work over the weekend and tell customer service he won't have the solution on Monday.
   - Reggie can explain that he thinks that they are in the best position to solve the problem without saying anything negative about Sandy and Mike.
   - Reggie can tell them that Sandy and Mike aren't very good programmers, and that's why he isn't asking them to work on the problem.
4. Answers will vary. The third solution listed above is best. Reggie can explain that he thinks that they are the people who can best solve this problem. In this way he will show that he is not punishing Chandra, Howard, and Jeannette, but asking for them to make an extra effort because he thinks so highly of them.
5. Answers will vary. Many people will feel that by praising employees whenever they do a good job, he can make sure they know that they are valued.
6. Answers will vary.

LESSON 1

Example
1. He hadn't stated the topic of the paragraph.
2. He thought readers should know that copywriters helped revise each other's drafts.
3. He thought the fact that one copywriter thought teleconferencing would help was unimportant or not related to the topic.

Exercise 1
1. Not all jobs are equally suited to telecommuting. Yes, it is stated clearly.
2. No, all of the ideas in the paragraph are not about the topic. Sentences 3 and 6 are not on the topic and should be cut.
3. Sentence 6 might serve as a transition to the next paragraph.

Exercise 2
Answers will vary.

LESSON 2

Example
1. He wanted to be more specific about the way telecommuting helped the environment. The change also makes the sentence more concise.
2. He wanted to present his ideas in a more logical order, relating the cause to its effects.
3. He wanted to be more specific and less wordy.
4. He wanted to be more concise.
5. The word he took out was not needed.

6. Yes. By taking out unnecessary words, being more specific, and arranging his ideas more logically, Reggie makes it easier for readers to follow what he wants to say.

Exercise 1

Answers will vary. Possible answers include:

1. Reggie probably did not mean *flexible,* but *open* in sentence 7.
2. Reggie could have stated the specific *people* he meant in sentence 6.
3. Reggie did not include any overused words or phrases.
4. The tone of sentence 7, especially the term *crazy hours* does not seem right for the audience.
5. Sentence 4 does not contain a complete idea. Sentences will vary.
6. Sentence 6 is not clear. Sentences will vary.
7. All sentences contain both a subject and a verb.
8. The verb *send* in sentence 3 is in the present tense while the rest of the paragraph is the past tense.

Exercise 2

Answers will vary.

LESSON 3

Exercise 1

The proofread paragraph should read as follows:

The experiment met with few technical problems. All telecommuters were lent computers, and some people had trouble setting them up. Breakdowns were rare, however, and they seldom had a serious impact on the work. Employees who had not worked on computers before found that it took time to learn how to use e-mail. Therefore, early in the experiment, these employees sometimes "lost" their work. However, after this start-up period, everything went very smoothly.